Baishali Bal

Drug, Sex, HIV and Street Children in India

HIV and Street Children

LAP LAMBERT Academic Publishing

Impressum/Imprint (nur für Deutschland/ only for Germany)
Bibliografische Information der Deutschen Nationalbibliothek: Die Deutsche Nationalbibliothek
verzeichnet diese Publikation in der Deutschen Nationalbibliografie; detaillierte bibliografische
Daten sind im Internet über http://dnb.d-nb.de abrufbar.
 Alle in diesem Buch genannten Marken und Produktnamen unterliegen warenzeichen-, marken-
oder patentrechtlichem Schutz bzw. sind Warenzeichen oder eingetragene Warenzeichen der
jeweiligen Inhaber. Die Wiedergabe von Marken, Produktnamen, Gebrauchsnamen,
Handelsnamen, Warenbezeichnungen u.s.w. in diesem Werk berechtigt auch ohne besondere
Kennzeichnung nicht zu der Annahme, dass solche Namen im Sinne der Warenzeichen- und
Markenschutzgesetzgebung als frei zu betrachten wären und daher von jedermann benutzt
werden dürften.

Coverbild: www.ingimage.com

Verlag: LAP LAMBERT Academic Publishing GmbH & Co. KG
Dudweiler Landstr. 99, 66123 Saarbrücken, Deutschland
Telefon +49 681 3720-310, Telefax +49 681 3720-3109
Email: info@lap-publishing.com

Herstellung in Deutschland:
Schaltungsdienst Lange o.H.G., Berlin
Books on Demand GmbH, Norderstedt
Reha GmbH, Saarbrücken
Amazon Distribution GmbH, Leipzig
ISBN: 978-3-8433-5105-8

Imprint (only for USA, GB)
Bibliographic information published by the Deutsche Nationalbibliothek: The Deutsche
Nationalbibliothek lists this publication in the Deutsche Nationalbibliografie; detailed
bibliographic data are available in the Internet at http://dnb.d-nb.de.
 Any brand names and product names mentioned in this book are subject to trademark, brand
or patent protection and are trademarks or registered trademarks of their respective holders.
The use of brand names, product names, common names, trade names, product descriptions
etc. even without a particular marking in this works is in no way to be construed to mean that
such names may be regarded as unrestricted in respect of trademark and brand protection
legislation and could thus be used by anyone.

Cover image: www.ingimage.com

Publisher: LAP LAMBERT Academic Publishing GmbH & Co. KG
Dudweiler Landstr. 99, 66123 Saarbrücken, Germany
Phone +49 681 3720-310, Fax +49 681 3720-3109
Email: info@lap-publishing.com

Printed in the U.S.A.
Printed in the U.K. by (see last page)
ISBN: 978-3-8433-5105-8

ACKNOWLEDGEMENT

A journey will be trouble-free or effortless when you travel together. Interdependence is more valuable than independence. This thesis is the result of two and half years of hard work whereby I have been accompanied and supported by many people. It is a pleasant memory that I have now the opportunity to express my gratitude for all of them.

The first person I would like to express my deep and sincere gratitude is my supervisor **Dr. Kamalesh Sarkar** M.D, Division of Epidemiology (HIV/AIDS), National Institute of Cholera & Enteric Diseases (NICED), Kolkata. I have been working under Dr. Sarkar in different projects of HIV/AIDS since 2002 till date. During the period I came to know about his overly enthusiasm and fundamental view on research and his mission for providing only high-quality work, which has made a deep impression on me. I owe him lots of gratitude for having me shown this way of research. He could not even realize how much I have learned from him. His wide knowledge and logical way of thinking have been of great value for me. His understanding, encouragement and personal guidance have provided a good basis for the completion of my thesis.

I owe my most sincere gratitude to our Director **Dr. G. B. Nair**, PhD and our former Director **Dr. S. K. Bhattacharya**, M.D, National Institute of Cholera & Enteric Diseases (NICED), who supported me with necessary permission for availing the opportunity using infrastructure (Laboratory, Library etc) of this institute for completion of my work. They also provided backing along with the field staffs during my difficult moments of fieldwork.

I passionately thank to **Dr. Rupa Mitra**, Senior Medical Officer of B.R.Sing Hospital, Indian Railways, for her valuable advice and friendly help. I am also thankful to the staffs of the Department of Maintenance, Eastern Railways for their whole-hearted support & cooperation to identify and approach the street children during field survey.
I also warmly thank to **Dr. Sujit Mallick**, Medical Officer of Eastern Indian Railways. His kind support was of great value in this study.

i

I sincerely thank all the **NGOs** (Saltlake Health Initiative for Necessary Environment, CINI Asha, Society for Community Intervention & Research, Medical Bank-Hatkhola, Bhoruka Blood Bank, Sethbagan Mahila Sangha, HIVE-India etc.) for extending their full cooperation in getting my study participants. I am really thankful to all my **Study Participants** without whose support & cooperation, this mammoth task would have never been possible.

I deeply thank to **Mr. Aiyel Haque Mallick**, Data Manager, HIV/AIDS Unit, National Institute of Cholera & Enteric Diseases (NICED), for his constant guidance & support for managing data of this work in a scientific way including necessary assistance for statistical analysis.

The chain of my gratitude would be definitely incomplete if I would forget to thank all of my colleagues. During this fieldwork, a team comprising of **Dr. Nabomita Roy**, Senior Research Fellow (Medical); **Ms. Debasree Chatterjee**, (Field Worker); **Mr. Mozaffar Hossain**, (Field Worker) and **Mr. Sanjoy Maity**, (Field Attendant) had been working under my supervision. I extend my sincere gratitude to all of them for their support.

I cannot end without thanking my family. I feel a deep sense of gratitude for my **parents** who formed my vision and high-quality thinking that really matters in my life. They have a tireless effort and constant encouragement to give a shape to my dream. They still are providing a persistent inspiration for my journey in this life.

CONTENTS

INTRODUCTION

The problem of 'street children' has been documented in many parts of the world since long back. Ancient history has also viewed and described street children in various ways. In 1848 Lord Ashley referred to more than 30,000 'naked, filthy, roaming lawless and deserted children', in and around London (DelCol, 1848). By 1922 there were at least 7 million homeless children in Russia as a result of nearly a decade of devastation from World War I and the Russian Civil War (Ball, 1998). Abandoned children formed gangs, created their own argot, and engaged in petty theft and prostitution. Examples from popular fiction include Kipling's "Kim" as a street child in colonial India, and Gavroche in Victor Hugo's Les Misérables. Fagin's crew of child pickpockets in "Oliver Twist" as well as Sherlock Holmes's "Baker Street Irregulars" attest to the presence of street children in 19th-century London.

Today also most civil societies view street children as an unwanted section; even they are not treated as members of a particular racial, ethnic, or religious group. Often street children were marked as anti-social and for their anti-social behavior, these children are viewed with suspicion and fear by civilians who would simply like to see the society free from them (Mervyn, 2002). These children are also exploited in their work place either because they are too young and therefore vulnerable to be working or because their working conditions are unsafe and exploitative. These unfortunate children thus lose their health, normal childhood and perhaps everything.

Street children are typically referred to children who need to survive alone on the street with or without link with their families. UNICEF has defined street children in three ways: *street living children* - who may have lost their parents and now, live alone on the street; *street working children* are children who spend most of their time working on the street or market for their livelihood and *street family children* who live on the street with their families (UNICEF, 2009). Almost all the country faces the problem of street children who are between the ages of 6 to 18 years. Estimated number of street children, who are struggling for food, shelter and proper clothing, vary between 100 million and 150 million worldwide (UNICEF, Rapid Assessment of Street Children In Lusaka, March,2002). India is the native land to the world's largest population of street children with an estimated 18 million children (CNN, 1998).

The term street children includes children who might not necessarily be homeless or without families, but who live in situations where there is no protection, supervision, or direction from responsible adults (HumanRightsWatch, 1996). Because of that, other members of the society

2

often harass them and throughout the world they are subjected to physical abuse by police as well as by the member of our civil society. In most of the country, governments treat them as a blight to be eradicated-rather than as children to be nurtured and protected (E.M.Salem & F.AbdEl.latif, 2002). Most of the children are criminally charged by police with vague offences such as loitering, vagrancy, or petty crime. These children are tormented and harassed by police and often confined for long periods in remand homes or lockups without showing any reason, only because they are homeless, unsupervised and lack autonomy (Reza, Kumar &Ahmmed, 2005). These street children are sometimes sexually abused, forced into sexual acts, or raped by adult members of the society (UNICEF, 2001). There is an alarming tendency by some law enforcement personnel and civilians, business proprietors and their private security firms, to view street children as almost sub-human. In many countries, the public has overwhelmingly negative view towards street children. They also support Government views to get these children off the street (Human Rights Watch, 1998).

Children were brought to streets for variety of reasons - Poverty, family disintegration, death of parents, abandon, orphaned or disowned by their parents. Neglect by other family members in absence of parents, exploitation by adults, sexual abuse by close family members, social unrest and natural disasters are perhaps the most common cause which increases the population of street children. Moreover, in developing countries, urbanization leads to migration of families to city that result in loss of family values and morals. Similarly, modernization is also a curse to this defenseless section of the society. As a result, innocent children are perhaps the greatest victims of this disintegration of social structure.

Street children generally lack parental guidance and supervision. Even those who have family attachments are often deprived from love, affection and family bonding. Rather they are often victims of family violence. Poverty, starvation and struggle for mere survival often force these poor children to the streets in search of a better living. The financial constraints of families of street children often push their male children to find a way to support their families economically and at the same time teaching their female children to tackle household situations. Deprived of their childhood, these children often become detached from their families and find solace in the freedom of living on the streets.

The social phenomenon of street children is increasing as the world's population grows. They often engage to petty theft and prostitution for their survival. They are extremely vulnerable to

3

sexually transmitted diseases including HIV/AIDS. Most of them start addiction to cope up with their stressful situation by inhalation of glue and paint thinner, which cause kidney failure, irreversible brain damage and mere death in some cases. There are some other reasons, which lead to the existence of street children in the developing countries. The first and foremost factor is urban poverty that leads to a breakdown of family and moral values. Some street children come from peculiar families where children are abused or neglected by the family members and finally street children are resulted from the adverse effects of modernization.

Street children frequently move between the streets and their homes on the basis of the changing family dynamics, the availability of friends on the streets, the degree of police harassment and the comparative economic conditions of the home and the streets. Children, who are not abandoned, almost always leave home in a measured manner, initially staying away for a night or two, then step-by-step spending more time away from home. Gradually they start spending more amount of time with other children. Generally these children do not completely ignore their family ties and even try to contribute a portion of their earning to their families. Commonly it is seen that they rarely break total family ties. Most of the children maintain frequent contact with their families and try to bear financial responsibility being a part of the family.

The problem of street children appears to be a global issue today. The phenomenon of street children & related problem is alarming and escalating globally. No country and virtually no city anywhere in the world today are without the presence of street children. It is a problem of both developed and developing countries, but it is more prevalent in the poor nations of Latin America, Asia and Africa.

In the Central Asian republics including Kazakhstan, Kyrgyz Republic, Tajikistan, and Uzbekistan and Mongolia, the presence of street children is a comparatively recent phenomenon which is closely associated with the collapse of the Soviet Union and the rapid transition to market-based economies. It is a new phenomenon especially in the Kyrgyz Republic (World Street Children News, 2001). It is the result of alcoholism of parents, poverty, exploitation, abuse, and domestic violence. Often the children have stepfathers or stepmothers who force children to leave home. These countries have experienced an increase in the number of street children who are at increased risk of being abused. They are subjected to violence not only by adults but also by their peers. Every day for them is a struggle for mere existence (West, Street Children in Asia and the Pacific, 2003). These children were subjected to the everyday risk of being abused, and experience violence at the hands of both adults and their peers and they have to struggle day-by-day to make a living.

South Asia is the home to some of the largest concentrations of street children. In this sub-region, street children have been stigmatized considered as a distinct social underclass for a longer period than elsewhere. Poverty again is the major contributing cause of street children across South Asia. It seems that intra-family conflict, abuse, and violence are most common leading causes for children's separation from family (West, 2003). Children's life on the streets of South Asia is characterized by discrimination and stigma, as well as problems of police harassment. Such harassment extends to illegal detention, detention on false charges, beatings and torture. Judicial system of most under developed countries is conceivably unable to help these children since most of legislations are outdated.

Afghanistan occupies a special position in the sub-region because due to its geographical location it serves as a bridge between East and Central Asia. In Afghanistan, the emergence of large numbers of street children is the consequence of more than two decades of armed conflict rather than the demise of the Soviet Union and economic transition. A preliminary head count in early 2002 recorded more than 37,000 children working and begging on the streets of Kabul.

According to the estimation of Asian Development Bank, about 25 million children are living on the streets in Asia (West, 2003). Among Asian countries, India occupies a prominent position with the world's largest concentration of street children (West, 2003). Moreover, in India cultural variations, intensity of abuse, maltreatment and violence among these children are increasing daily (Reza, Kumar, & Ahmmed, 2005) Kolkata, one of the four major metropolitan cities of the country, has an estimated number of 10,714 street children (Lipovsek, 2007). Most of these children, though not rootless or unattached, remain unsupervised by adults. Majority of them are found to be employed in some kind of work to support themselves or their families. They work as porters, vendors, shoe-shiners, street tailors, newspaper sellers, rag pickers, coolies, store helpers, sales persons, parking attendants etc (Ganeshan, 1996), (Reza, Kumar, & Ahmmed, 2005).

A large number of families are found to live on pavements, under flyovers, car parking places and many street children are seen to spend nights on open streets in Kolkata. Some children

5

spend their days on the street but are able to return home at night; but others have no home to return to and they have to sleep anywhere they find shelter. Majority of them are found to be working for survival. Deprived of childhood, education, proper shelter, basic food and a good future, a large number of street children in West Bengal, especially in Kolkata, are found to victim of HIV/AIDS and Sexually Transmitted Infections (STIs) through regular sexual exploitation and addiction to different substances.

Street children because of their poor living conditions are easy victims of sexual abuses among themselves as well as by adults. Sexual abuse of a child is defined as, "the involvement of a child in sexual activity that he/she does not fully comprehend and not in the position to give informed consent or that violate the laws or social taboos of society" (Forster & Tannhauser, 1996). When a child is used or attempted to be used for sexual stimulation by any means by others who is in position or power to control over the victim at least once within last one year was considered as sexual abuse. Sexual abuse occurs in rural, urban and suburban areas and almost in all ethnic, racial and socio-economic groups (Abuse, 1994). Government of India admitted that the numbers of Indian street children are raising all over the country and it is coming to the world's largest population of street children. About 53% children were reported to have sexually abused in a study of ministry of women & child development in India. Assam, Delhi, Andhra Pradesh, and Bihar reported the highest incidence of sexual abuse among street children. Recently, West Bengal has documented about 55% sexual abuses among street based children (AsiaOneNews, 2009). As well as WHO report says that globally 8% of boys and 25% of girls below 18 year suffer from sexual abuse in every year (WHO, 2002). Child sexual abuse has a long term effect on their psychological, social and mental well-being. Some of them suffer from psychiatric trauma (Finkelhor, Gerald, & Hotaling & Kersti, 1988) and social functioning problems resulting from feelings of powerlessness, guilt, shame and low self esteem (Finkelhor D, 1986), (Boyer & Fine, 1992) that reduces their ability to protect further abuse. Even the physical force used in sexual abuse may result in extensive injuries in genital tract which may facilitate transmission of sexually transmitted diseases (STDs). A study in Delhi revealed that 25% of such adolescent suffer from STDs (Pandhi, Khama, & Sekhri, 1995), (JAMA, 1985), (Pinto & Ruff, 1994). Moreover they are considered to play an important role in spreading HIV/STIs and have been categorized under bridging population for spreading HIV, Hepatitis B & C in the community as evident by several studies (Sarkar, Das, & Panda, 1993), (Sarkar, Mitra, & Bal, 2003), (Sarkar, Bal, & Mukherjee, 2006).

Like sexual abuse, street children are vulnerable to substance abuse also. Substance abuse is mostly viewed as a common phenomenon among street children of India. The non-medical use of chemical substances in order to achieve alterations in physical or mental functioning has been termed as substance abuse (Merrill & Peters, 2001). WHO estimates that globally, 25% to 90% of street children indulge in substance abuses (WHO, Child Abuse and Neglect, 1997). Many behavioral as well as health issues are associated with substance/drug abuse of street children. These are violence, stealing, telling lies or being sexually abused to get the substances and some diseases particularly blood borne infections, malnutrition etc. Another important issue that may result from substance abuse is transmission of HIV/AIDS through injecting drug use. The state of West Bengal, earlier known to be a low HIV prevalent state, has already entered into a medium prevalent state for HIV as per criteria specified by National AIDS Control Organization (NACO). Kolkata, the capital city of West Bengal, is close to high HIV prevalent zone as revealed by a recent study carried out by National Institute of Cholera and Enteric Diseases (NICED) with collaboration of West Bengal State AIDS Prevention & Control Society (WBSACS) (Sarkar, Bal, & Mukherjee, 2005).

On the other hand, street children are considered as one of the bridging population and because of their vulnerability to sexual and substance abuse, they may play a vital role in spreading HIV in the community. Moreover, evidence suggests that the number of street children is increasing day by day particularly in a metropolitan city like Kolkata but research activities and related data are not enough in this field for government information and taking necessary actions.

Considering all these factors, studying street children has been considered as a felt need of the present time and possible intervention measures are required to be taken up to stop further spread of HIV and STIs in the community. With the background of dearth of reliable data on magnitude of problem of street children, socio-demography, risk behavior, risk perceptions and their vulnerability to HIV/STIs, which are required for designing a successful intervention programme towards them, the present study was carried out.

OBJECTIVES:
1. To study the prevalence of non-tobacco substance abuse among street children
2. To study the prevalence of sexual abuse in the said population
3. To study their socio-demography

7

4. To study the factor/s that are likely to be associated with sexual and substance abuse

5. To study their blood- borne infections & Sexually Transmitted Infections (STIs)

REVIEW OF LITERATURE

A study on street children was conducted in Delhi by **Dr. Deepti Pagare** in 2004 to study the risk factors of substance abuse. The study was conducted among 115 male street children. More than half (57.4%) of the subjects were found to indulge in substance abuse. The agents consumed by them were nicotine (44.5%), inhalants (24.3%), alcohol (21.8%) etc. This study significantly found that substance use in street children was associated with unstable homes and maltreatment.

Deepti Pagare (2005) from Maulana Azad Medical college, Delhi was carried out a study by 189 street children aged 6-18 years. She observed that majority of them (38.1%) had suffered from sexual abuse. On clinical examination, 61.1% showed physical signs and 40.2% showed behavioural signs of sexual abuse. Forcible sex was reported by 44.4% of victims and 25% reported to have sexually transmitted diseases. Author realized that identification of victims and their proper rehabilitation (medical, social & psychological) would be the only prevention of further abuse of street children.

S. Khurana (2004) reported Mental Health Status of Runaway Adolescents in Delhi and found that out of 150 street children, 38% was abused physically and 14.6% was sexually abused. About 94.7% physically abused children gave history of physical abuse by family member and 5.3% by their relatives, friends and unknown people on streets.

S. Khurana (2004) reported from a study that 55.3% of the study participants (N=150) had any history of substance abuse. A wide range of substance abuse was elicited, 49.6% of children gave history of tobacco intake. Glue sniffing was reported by 2.66% of cases and 0.67% reported ganja intake. That study explained the prevalence of substance abuse was high among runaway and homeless youth.

Abinash Rai (2002) a researcher, illustrated that in Nepal one in ten teenagers was drug addict. Of these 56% smoke, 26% inhale and 5.6% inject. Researchers estimated that all crime was drug related. According to that study, carried out with 118 street children, different substances used by them were: cigarette-72.9%, tobacco- 18.6%, alcohol- 30.5%, marijuana-30.5%, tidigesic-3.4% and dendrite- 51.7%. Majority of them (95.1%) used to glue sniffing with their friends.

Tyler KA (2004) explained a study on Risk factors for sexual victimization among male & female homeless and runaway youths from an university of USA. He remarked that homeless female street living children were associated with sexual victimization by both stranger or friends and those who were engaged in more high risk behaviours were expected to be at greater risk for sexual victimization. In this study, out of 372 participants, 35% had been sexually victimized.

Rew L (2001) from USA, explored that homeless youths have high rates of sexual abuse and abuse of alcohol and other drugs. That study was carried out among 96 homeless youths. Over 60% of the sample reported a history of sexual abuse and majority was under the age of 12 years when they tried alcohol, marijuana, cocain, injecting drugs first time. The author in this study realized that high prevalence of sexual abuse among homeless youths needs to develop a community based intervention to improve their health status.

Lewis Aptekar (1994) from San Jose State University, pointed out that why street children were from some cultural background and not from others. The reasons for their existence were related to poverty, abuse, and modernizing factors.

Ahmadkhaniha HR (2007) from Iran University of Medical sciences, studied the frequency of sexual abuse and depression among 87 street children of Tehran. Among them 20.9% (n=18) children was sexually abused. It was observed that, 26 girls (86.7%) and 27 boys (48.2%) suffered from depression and depressed children were 3.2 times more likely to be sexually abused than non-depressed children.

Susan S Serman (2006) has given explanation on drug use, street survival & risk behaviour among street children in Lahor. An estimated number of 3,500–5,000 street children are living on the streets of Lahore, Pakistan. Drug use is a major coping mechanism among street children in Lahore and is associated with many behaviors.

About 17.0% reported never having used drugs, 15.9% reported that they were former drug users and 67.1% reported about using drugs during the time of registration.

Anthony K. Wutoh (2005) has conducted a survey among 100 street children aged 11–19 years and collected data on HIV knowledge, risk behaviors, home and sexual experiences, and factors that contributed to their relocation to the street environment in Takoradi, Ghana. 80% of the street children had at least minimal knowledge of HIV and 54% perceived themselves to be at risk for contracting HIV.

11

study the risk factors of substance abuse. The study was conducted among 115 male street children. More than half (57.4%) of the subjects were found to indulge in substance abuse. The agents consumed by them were nicotine (44.5%), inhalants (24.3%), alcohol (21.8%) etc. This study significantly found that substance use in street children was associated with unstable homes and maltreatment.

Deepti Pagare (2005) from Maulana Azad Medical college, Delhi was carried out a study by 189 street children aged 6-18 years. She observed that majority of them (38.1%) had suffered from sexual abuse. On clinical examination, 61.1% showed physical signs and 40.2% showed behavioural signs of sexual abuse. Forcible sex was reported by 44.4% of victims and 25% reported to have sexually transmitted diseases. Author realized that identification of victims and their proper rehabilitation (medical, social & psychological) would be the only prevention of further abuse of street children.

S. Khurana (2004) reported Mental Health Status of Runaway Adolescents in Delhi and found that out of 150 street children, 38% was abused physically and 14.6% was sexually abused. About 94.7% physically abused children gave history of physical abuse by family member and 5.3% by their relatives, friends and unknown people on streets.

S. Khurana (2004) reported from a study that 55.3% of the study participants (N=150) had any history of substance abuse. A wide range of substance abuse was elicited, 49.6% of children gave history of tobacco intake. Glue sniffing was reported by 2.66% of cases and 0.67% reported ganja intake. That study explained the prevalence of substance abuse was high among runaway and homeless youth.

 Abinash Rai (2002) a researcher, illustrated that in Nepal one in ten teenagers was drug addict. Of these 56% smoke, 26% inhale and 5.6% inject. Researchers estimated that all crime was drug related. According to that study, carried out with 118 street children, different substances used by them were: cigarette-72.9%, tobacco- 18.6%, alcohol- 30.5%, marijuana- 30.5%, tidigesic-3.4% and dendrite- 51.7%. Majority of them (95.1%) used to glue sniffing with their friends.

Tyler KA (2004) explained a study on Risk factors for sexual victimization among male & female homeless and runaway youths from an university of USA. He remarked that homeless female street living children were associated with sexual victimization by both stranger or friends and those who were engaged in more high risk behaviours were expected to be at

12

greater risk for sexual victimization. In this study, out of 372 participants, 35% had been sexually victimized.

Rew L (2001) from USA, explored that homeless youths have high rates of sexual abuse and abuse of alcohol and other drugs. That study was carried out among 96 homeless youths. Over 60% of the sample reported a history of sexual abuse and majority was under the age of 12 years when they tried alcohol, marijuana, cocain, injecting drugs first time. The author in this study realized that high prevalence of sexual abuse among homeless youths needs to develop a community based intervention to improve their health status.

Lewis Aptekar (1994) from San Jose State University, pointed out that why street children were from some cultural background and not from others. The reasons for their existence were related to poverty, abuse, and modernizing factors.

Ahmadkhaniha HR (2007) from Iran University of Medical sciences, studied the frequency of sexual abuse and depression among 87 street children of Tehran. Among them 20.9% (n=18) children was sexually abused. It was observed that, 26 girls (86.7%) and 27 boys (48.2%) suffered from depression and depressed children were 3.2 times more likely to be sexually abused than non-depressed children.

Susan S Serman (2006) has given explanation on drug use, street survival & risk behaviour among street children in Lahor. An estimated number of 3,500–5,000 street children are living on the streets of Lahore, Pakistan. Drug use is a major coping mechanism among street children in Lahore and is associated with many behaviors. About 17.0% reported never having used drugs, 15.9% reported that they were former drug users and 67.1% reported about using drugs during the time of registration.

Anthony K. Wutoh (2005) has conducted a survey among 100 street children aged 11–19 years and collected data on HIV knowledge, risk behaviors, home and sexual experiences, and factors that contributed to their relocation to the street environment in Takoradi, Ghana. 80% of the street children had at least minimal knowledge of HIV and 54% perceived themselves to be at risk for contracting HIV.

Pagare D (2004) explained the risk factors of substance abuse among street children from Delhi. A total of 115 children were interviewed at the time of their admission in a observation home. He reported that substance use in street children was associated with unstable homes

13

and maltreatment and more than half of them had indulged in substance abuse before coming to the observation home.

Huang CC (2004) conducted a comparative study of abandoned street children and formerly abandoned street children in La Paz, Bolivia. The attitude was different among children who have already entered into orphanage compared to those who didn't get any guidence.

Ali M (2005) carried out a study first time in Pakistan to elicit street children's perceptions of health and the barriers to service utilization. These youth were highly susceptible to many adverse health outcomes like injuries, respiratory and skin infections etc. Self-medication was preferred instead of taking treatment from public or private medical sector. They perceived constraints to services including long waiting time, monetary, negative attitude of service providers and their inferior status. They prefer user-friendly services that would be sensitively dealt with street children's needs and requirements.

Dooan MC (2006) conducted a study in Turkey to determine the oral health status of street children. Street children were commonly faced with oral health problems, especially periodontal problems. Oral health policies and preventive services including oral health promotion programmes were essential. It can give information about dental issues and can make positive changes in behavioural and environmental factors. The priority should be to control the factors which result in the occurrence of new dental problems.

Vahdani P (2006) reported about the prevalence of Hepatitis B, Hepatitis C, Human Immunodeficiency Virus infection among street children in Southern Tehran, Iran. He studied 39 (38%) boys and 63 (62%) girls, including 79 (77%) Afghan and 16 (16%) Iranian children. The children were negative for syphilis, HIV, and HCV. Nevertheless, 3 of them were positive for HBsAg and 15 were HBsAb positive (>10 MIU/mL). The majority of street children were immigrants. Although these children did not have syphilis, HIV, and HCV, they were at risk of HBV due to their risky behaviours.

Pinzon-Randon AM (2006) He explained that child labor in the streets was a dangerous activity characterized by long working hours and exposure to risk factors. Child work has different characteristics in each of the cities, which suggested that the solution to the problem must be designed on a case by case basis.

Greksa LP (2007) Studied 150 poor street children who live & work on the street to assess the effect of street life on the growth and health status of poor children who live and work full-time on the streets of Dhaka, Bangladesh. The greater-than-expected growth and health status of street children, compared to other poor children, may be due to biologically fitter children being more likely to permanently move to the streets and/or to remain on the streets once the move has been made.

Richter MS (2007) A profound researchers, investigated social and economic determinants of health often interact with vulnerable and marginalized populations. The participants in that study lacked the age of majority and were without any legal guardian. The researchers experienced considerable difficulty in obtaining ethical approval to conduct the study. The street children, at first, were not allowed to give informed consent for the study because of their minor age. Ethical principles of autonomy, disclosure, competence and understanding, consent and voluntariness, beneficence and non-maleficence, and justice are described and applied to this case study involving street children in a South African neighbourhood. It is suggested that by working within an ethical framework, the safety of research participants will be assured and the quality of the research will be enhanced.

Ahmadkhaniha HR (2007) explained the frequency of sexual abuse and depression among street children lived in a deprived district of Tehran. About 20.9% of the children had been sexually abused. Depressed children were 3.2 times more likely to be sexually abused than non-depressed children. Furthermore, 86.7% girls (n=26) and 48.2% boys (n=27) suffered from depression. The frequency of depression demonstrated a significant association with the father's or breadwinner's history of imprisonment or unemployment. Interventional programs providing education and support should be implemented for street children.

Kissim DM (2007) Has documented HIV sero-prevalence among street youth in St Petersburg and described the social, sexual, and behavioral characteristics associated with HIV infection. Out of 313 participants, 117 (37.4%, 95% confidence interval 26.1-50.2%) were HIV infected. Most HIV-infected street youth (96.6%) were sexually active; they had multiple partners (65.0%), and used condoms (80.3%) inconsistently. Street youth aged 15-19 years in St Petersburg , Russia , have an extraordinarily high HIV seroprevalence. In street youth who are injection drug users, HIV seroprevalence is the highest ever reported for eastern Europe and is among the highest in the world.

Olgar S (2008) has studied that substance abuse was prevalent in adolescent street children, and death was reported as secondary to aspiration, accidental trauma, asphyxia, cardiac arrhythmia, anoxia, vagal inhibition and respiratory depression. Echocardiography revealed increased diameters of the left ventricle and atrium, the aorta, and the coronary arteries as compared to the healthy children (p less than 0.05).

Worthman CM (2008) in a study suggested a need for critical appraisal of homelessness and migration as a risk factor to youth, given prevailing local conditions such as rural poverty, and represents the only multidimensional study of childhood allostatic load and developmental risk in non-Western settings.

Kahabuka FK (2006) explained a level of knowledge on causes and prevention of dental caries and bleeding gums, oral hygiene and eating practices among institutionalized former street children. Eighty-eight per cent and 83% of the children knew the cause of tooth decay and bleeding gums respectively and 17-68% were aware of preventive measures. About 92% of the children said they brush their teeth but 74% brushed when living on the streets, this difference was significant (chi2=4.40, P=0.05).The findings of this study has shown that most former street children are aware of the causes of dental caries and bleeding gums but have poor knowledge on prevention of the two diseases. Furthermore, children living on the streets are more likely to eat cariogenic foods and have poor oral hygiene practices.

Connolly M (1993) has estimated that of 100 million 5-18 year street children have been facing sexual risks in urban areas worldwide. About 70% were on the streets, during the day and returned home at night and 20-25% knew where their families were, but preferred to live on the streets. About 5-10% was without family and had to live on the streets. About 25-33% was young girls. Poverty was one of the driving forces for street children from rural areas. These children faced illnesses such as respiratory infections, skin diseases, gastrointestinal problems, trauma, sexual abuse, exploitation, unwanted pregnancy, and sexually transmitted diseases, such as syphilis and gonorrhea. Many of them faced violence followed by death. As the numbers of street children have grown, the need of necessary health services have increased.

MATERIALS & METHODS

Following definitions were used for this study:

Street Children:

Children who might not necessarily be homeless or without families, but who live in situations where there is no protection, supervision, or direction from responsible adults **(Danilo).** According to this definition, street children have been categorized by UNICEF as follows:

1. Who may have lost their parents & now live alone on the street.
2. Who spend most of their time working on the street for their livelihood and
3. Who live on the street with their families

Substance abuse:

History of intake through oral / sublingual / injection / inhalation / contact with skin or mucous membrane of any substance/s for non medical purpose/s (such as elevating mood, to overcome depression, to get energy) at least once/week for two consecutive weeks within last three months from the date of interview was considered as substance abuse for this study. Substance abuse was considered when s/he is reported to have abused one or more of the following:

1. Smoking of any type of tobacco.
2. Chewing any tobacco in form of gutkha, sikhar etc.
3. Ingestion of cough syrup containing morphin, codine etc.
4. Intake of chemical substances like Morphin, Pheniramine maleate (Avil), Buprenorphine (Tidigesic), Ibuprofen (Brufen) etc. through IV or IM or oral.
5. Intake of any other non-tobacco substance/s through any route for non medical purposes.

Non-tobacco substance abuse means consumption of any non-tobacco addictive substance/s with or without tobacco product/s.

Sexual Abuse:

Sexual abuse was measured in this study by using Finkelhor's scale to assess the detailed nature of the sexual exploitation faced by the child. A child is said to be sexually abused, when s/he reports the following that occurred with him/her within past six month:

1. Touched the subject in a disturbing way
2. Kissed/hugged which troubled the subject
3. Touched multiple parts of the subject forcefully
4. Forceful exposure of genitalia of the abuser to the subject
5. Forced the subject to expose his/her genitalia
6. Forced the subject to touch the genitalia of the abuser
7. Forcefully touched the genitalia of the subjects
8. Forcefully rubbed the subject
9. Tried to have sex with the subject
10. Had sex/ rape the subject

HIV positive:

HIV positive subjects are those who show the presence of HIV antibody in their blood tested at a qualified HIV testing laboratory.

Sexually Transmitted Infection (STIs):

A subject is known to be suffering from STIs if his/ her serum shows reactivity to VDRL test in 1:8 dilutions followed by TPHA as confirmatory test.

Study method:

It was a community based cross-sectional study. The study was conducted in Kolkata city focusing entire northern and adjacent part that constitutes almost half of the city (figure- 1). Selection of subjects was made by Conventional Cluster sampling technique for 'Hard-to-Reach' population **(Lipovsek & Longfield, 2007).** Mapping exercise done by West Bengal

20

State AIDS Prevention & Control Society (WBSACS) in collaboration with Department For International Development (DFID) that validated initially to make the sampling frame for this study and a list of primary sampling units (PSUs) was obtained **(DFID, 2003).**

Relevant local authorities (local police stations, NGOs/CBOs, ward offices of Kolkata Municipal Corporation wards, Divisional Railway Manager, Sealdah & Howrah Railway Stations etc.) were contacted and their co-operation was sought. Informed consent was obtained from the said authorities on behalf of study community considering the fact that most of the study participants do not have their legal guardians and as per advice of institutional ethical committee. Strict confidentiality was maintained.

Estimation of Sample size:

Considering an estimated street children population of 5000 (sampling frame), expected frequency of sexual abuse = 10% and absolute precision = 75%, the sample size was calculated to be 554. Considering a non participation rate of 3%, the final sample size for this study was calculated to be 570. Sample size was calculated using `STATCALC PROGRAMME' of Epi-Info soft ware, Version - 6.04d, developed by CDC, Atlanta, USA.

Creation of Sampling Frame:

In our study area (northern part of Kolkata city), street children were estimated to be 4994 by the West Bengal State AIDS Prevention & Control Society. A team from Division of Epidemiology (HIV/AIDS), National Institute of Cholera & Enteric Diseases revalidated this that resulted to 5000 estimated street children (approximately) spread over 50 clusters with variable number of study population within the study area. These clusters were considered as primary sampling Units (PSUs). Initially listing of all PSUs was made with their corresponding population size. Below (Table-1) is a structure of sampling frame with the measure of size of each selected Primary Sampling Units (PSUs).

Table: 1: Primary sampling units (PSUs) with Population size & selected PSUs

PSU No.	Description	Measure of size	Cumulative size	Cluster with PPS
1	Jatindra Mohan Av.	50	50	
2	Mitra Lane	180	230	
3	West Canal Road	110	340	X
4	Jan Bazar	20	360	
5	Canal East Rd.	18	378	
6	Ahiritola	78	456	
7	Gopal Mukherjee Road	180	636	
8	Bidhan Sarani	220	856	X
9	Rammohan Sarani	65	921	
10	Mechuya Bazar	26	947	
11	Rani Rasmoni Rd.	45	992	
12	Prem Chand St.	80	1072	
13	Baghbazar Ghat	60	1132	X
14	Manicktola More	80	1212	
15	Pagla Danga	112	1324	
16	C. R. Avenue	180	1504	
17	Park Circus More	140	1644	X
18	Kesab Ch. Sen St	210	1854	
19	B. K. Pal Avenue	48	1902	
20	Rafi Ahmd Kidwai Road	66	1968	X
21	Lake Town	75	2043	
22	Prachi Cinema	58	2101	
23	China Goli	44	2145	
24	C.R.Av.(Central Metro)	54	2199	
25	A. P. C Road	86	2285	

PSU No No.	Description	Measure of size	Cumulative size	Cluster with PPS
26	Phool Bagan More	21	2306	
27	Sealdah South	115	2421	X
28	Kashipur Road	92	2513	
29	Rabindra Sarani	98	2611	
30	Near Lady Brabourne	114	2725	
31	Paik Para	43	2768	
32	Sovabazar Metro	65	2833	X
33	Surya Sen Street	98	2931	
34	Sealdah Bus Stand	78	3009	
35	Dal Potti	79	3088	
36	Near Khanna Hall	122	3210	
37	Ultadanga Main Road	123	3333	X
38	Bidhan Sarani	115	3448	
39	B. B. Ganguly	120	3568	
40	Narkel Danga Bosti	125	3693	X
41	Beleghata More	200	3893	
42	Purabi Cinema	130	4023	
43	Posta Bazar	118	4141	X
44	Chaul Potti	76	4217	
45	Beadon Sr & Hedua	74	4291	
46	Santosh Mitra Sqare	145	4436	
47	Moulali	78	4514	X
48	Ganesh Takij	170	4684	
49	Arobindo Sarani	121	4805	
50	Raja Bazar More	189	4994	X
Cumulative Total= 4,994				

Considering a sample size of 570 and an average size of each cluster as 50, the required clusters would be =12 cluster (600/ 50 = 12). As the size of some clusters was much larger than others, so Probability Proportionate to Size (PPS) sampling was used for the selection of 12 clusters from the above sampling frame. These 12 clusters were selected after calculating a sampling interval of 416.16 (4994/12). Initially, a number of '300' was selected considering a random number between 1 to 416.16. This number was matching with the cumulative number of PSU 3 (see above table-1). So, the first selected sampling unit was 3. The second unit was selected by adding the arbitrary number with the sampling interval number that was 300+416.16= 716.16 which fell into the sampling unit no.8. The third one was selected by adding the sampling interval number with the total number getting in second step that was 416.16 + 716.16=1132.32. That procedure was followed until the list was completed. In this way, cluster numbers of 3, 8, 13, 17, 20, 27, 32, 37, 40, 43, 47 & 50 were selected (shown in the map of Kolkata city). Then average no. of 50 subjects was selected from each cluster randomly using random number table to cover required sample size.

Study area:

Kolkata is one of the four major metropolitan cities of India with 141 civic administrative units (NewWorldEncyclopedia, 2006). Out of 141 administrative units, a total of 64 units were covered the Northern part of Kolkata city (figure-1) where this study was proposed. The study was conducted within selected 12 clusters of these 64 civic administrative units with the help of field staff of NICED and local NGOs/CBOs working with street children in those areas. Kolkata, formerly called Calcutta, is the capital city of West Bengal. It is located on the east bank of the river Hooghly. Kolkata is one of the largest cities in India covering an area of 187 square km. with a population of more than 14.7 million (Sharma & Carl, 2007).

Figure-1: Map of Kolkata City showing study area (highlighted area) & selected PSUs

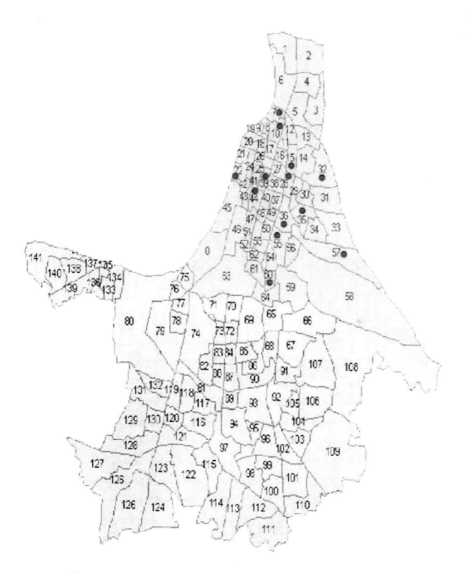

Study Population:

Children, that included street living, street working and street family children, who were found in different locations of Northern part of Kolkata city, were subjected as our study population.

Inclusion Criteria: 1. Children residing in study area of Kolkata.

2. Children willing to participate

3. Children in the age group of 6-18 years.

4. Children not seriously ill.

Exclusion Criteria: 1. Children residing outside study area.

2. Children unwilling to participate

3. Children under 6 year and over 18 years of age.

4. Seriously ill children.

Fieldwork:

The fieldwork was started with initial rapport building with the study participants through their parental, institutional or local authorities. After introducing, authorities as well as children were explained the purpose of the study and requested to assist/participate in this. All willing children were planned to include as participants with the support of their authorities. Following this, a questionnaire that was made for studying socio-demography, risk-behaviour and risk-perceptions, was structured and tested in the field. After initial field-testing, the said questionnaire was modified accordingly. The questionnaire was structured with combination of both open as well as close-ended questions for the easy understanding of all the participants. The participants were interviewed with the help of that pre-tested questionnaire to study their socio-demography, risk behaviour and risk perceptions etc. Questionnaire was printed in local language. Information was collected from each participant through face-to-face interview using local language. This was followed by collection of 3-4 ml. blood sample from all the study participants for studying the sero-prevalence of HIV, HBV, VDRL (1:8 dilutions) and TPHA (confirmatory test) in them. All the collected data was edited on the same day of collection. Following this, data was entered and analyzed in computer with the help of `Epi Info software, version 3.5.1.

Parameter studied: 1. Substance abuse

2. Sexual abuse

3. HIV infection

4. STIs indicated by VDRL (>= 1:8 dilution)

5. TPHA (confirmatory test)

6. Hepatitis-B (HBV) infection

Laboratory Procedure:

Blood samples were collected in vacutainer containing EDTA and transported to the Sexually Transmitted Infection (STI) laboratory as well as HIV laboratory of National Institute of Cholera & Enteric Diseases (NICED), Kolkata. HIV testing was done by ELISA followed by another rapid test (tri-dot test) as per national guidelines of HIV testing. ELISA tests were done by Vironostika HIV Uni-Form IIAg/Ab Microelisa System. The test was performed according to the manufacturer's (Biomerieux, Boseind-15, 5281 RM Boxtel, The Netherlands) instruction and samples reactive for tests were detected as positive for HIV. The ELISA reactive samples were then re-tested with another immuno-blot method known as 'HIV-TRI-DOT' as per instruction of its manufacturer (J. Mitra & Co. Ltd., New Delhi, India). Samples were also tested for VDRL (Venereal Diseases Research Laboratory) tests to determine syphilis serology as a composite indicator of Sexually Transmitted Infection STI). VDRL was considered as positive when the sample was reactive in 1:8 dilutions. All VDRL positive samples were retested by TPHA test. The samples positive with both VDRL as well as TPHA were considered as recently (old as well as new infections) infected with syphilis. HBV test was carried out by ELISA method.

Analysis of data:

Edited data was entered in computer using Epi-Info version 3.5.1. Analysis of data was done using the same software. Analysis was made to find out the distribution of socio-demographic variables like age, sex, education, occupation, marital status etc. as well as prevalence of substance and sexual abuse and factors those were likely to be associated with them.

Duration of the study: Three years.

OBSERVATIONS

A total of 570 street children were approached (who were eligible as per inclusion criteria) for this study. Of them, 554 (Five hundred and fifty four) street children participated in this study voluntarily (with a refusal rate of 2.8%) under guidance and supervision of their guardians/community leaders/care taker NGOs etc. These children were subjected to study their socio-demography, non-tobacco substance & sexual abuse pattern and factors that were likely to be associated with abuses.

A. Demography:

Age group-wise, majority was in the age group of 11-15 year (49.5%; n=274) followed by 15 years and above age group (36.8%; n=204). Youngest age group (6-10 year) was 13.7% (n=76). Median age of the study participants was 13 year [figure-2].

Figure 2: Age-wise distribution of studied participants (N=554)

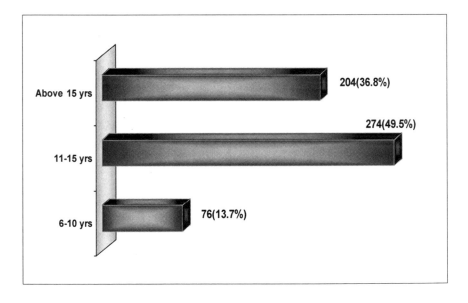

Median age: 13 year

Sex-wise, 65% (n=362) was male and 35% (n=192) was female children in this study (figure-3).

Figure 3: Sex distribution of studied participants (N=554)

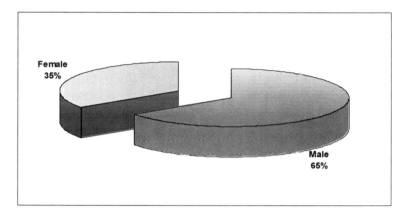

Education-wise, 40% (n=221) participants had some kind of formal education, and 13% (n=75) had non-formal education. About 47% (n=258) children was found to have neither formal nor non-formal education indicating illiterate children.

Figure 4: Educational status of studied participants (N=554)

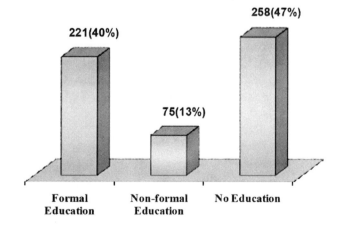

he term formal education refers to the structured educational system provided by the state or private organization for children. A formal education program is the process of training and developing people in knowledge, skills, mind, and character in a structured and certified program. On the other hand, non-formal education refers to education which takes place outside of the formally organized school. In this study, informal education means learning with the help of NGOs or related agencies with the aim of improving basic education of street children who do not have opportunities to attend school. Among children having formal education, most attended school up to the 5th standard then they dropped out sharply as shown in figure-5. It is evident from the figure that 13% attended class I, 16% up to class II, 19% attended up to class III, 13% attended class IV and 25% attended up to class V. Adding trend line, it clearly shows that there was sharp drop of formal schooling after reaching 4th standard (figure-5).

Figure 5: Distribution of formal education among street children (n=221)

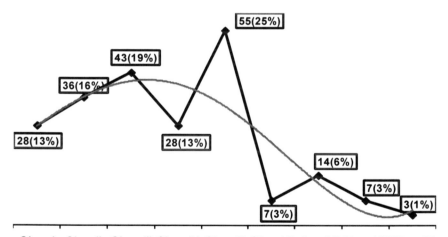

Class I   Class II   Class III   Class IV   Class V   Class VI   class VII   Class VIII   Class IX

On evaluation of ability to read and write, it was observed that children having formal education (40%; n=221) were able to read & write and rest (60%; n=333) were unable to do so.

So far marital status was concerned, 95% (n=342) of the male children and 67% (n=128) of the female children were never married. Only 4% of the male (n=16) and 30% of the female participants (n=58) were found to be married and living together. It was also interesting to note that few female and male children (3%; n=6 and 1%; n=4) were married but separated from each other [table-2].

Table-2: Marital status of street children (N=554)

Categories	Male (n=362)	Female (n=192)
Never Married	342 (95%)	128 (67%)
Married	16 (4%)	58 (30%)
Married but separated	4 (1%)	6 (3%)
Total:	362 (65%)	192 (35%)

Occupationally, most participants (72%; n=398) were found to engage in some kind of work to support themselves and/or their families. Only 28% (n=156) of them remained jobless at the time of this study as shown in figure-6.

Figure 6: Occupational status of studied participants (N=554)

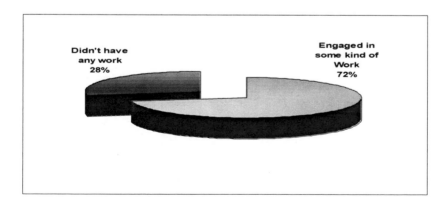

33

Table-3 shows about types of work done by the study participants. Most of the study participants (37.4%; n=149) were engaged in working with different types of small shops or hotels where they worked as a daily labour or helper. Other jobs included rag picking (19%; n=115), van pulling (16%; n=64) etc. Few of them were reported to be begging (6%; n=21) and stealing (7.3%; n=29) for their livelihood. It was also observed that a sizable number of children (5.8%; n=23) were engaged with dressing and packaging of fishes, mostly for exporting to some other places. Only 1 child was found to be involved in drug peddling.

Table-3: Types of work done by street children (n=398)

Types of Work	Frequency	Percentage (%)
Rag Picker	115	19%
Shop / Hotel worker / Labour	149	37.40%
Van puller	64	16%
Beggar	21	5.30%
Stealing	29	7.30%
Show game	5	1.20%
Fish Dressing	23	5.80%
Peddler	1	0.25%

Income distribution shows that majority (36%; n=145) had an income between Indian rupees of 500 to Rs.1000 per month [Indian Rs.50/- = US $ 1], followed by income of Rs.1001 to

34

Rs.1500 (29.4%; n=117) followed by income between Rs.2001 to Rs.3000 (13.3%; n=53). The highest monthly income was above Rs.5000 which 2% (n=7) of the participants had and 7% had the lowest monthly income of Rs.500 or less (figure-7).

Figure 7: Income distribution of study participants (N=554)

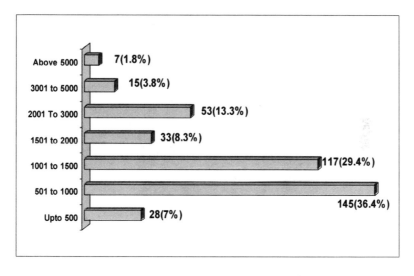

Most jobless (28%; n=156) children used to receive their financial support from their peer group and family members (94%) and about 6% of them (n=10) were reported to be supported by local NGOs as shown in figure-8.

Figure-8: Jobless children receiving supports from other sources (n=156)

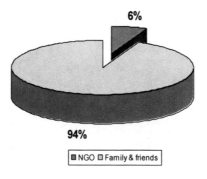

35

Study participants reported reason/s of involvement of their work. Most participants (68%; n=270) reported to do work to support themselves as well as their family members whereas, 32% of them (n=128) involved in work only to meet their daily needs (figure-9).

Figure-9: Response of street children about the involvement in work (n=398)

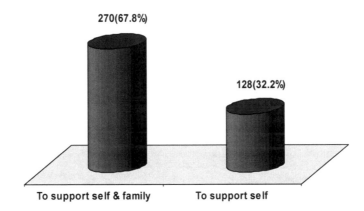

Parental supervision and guidance seem to be an important issue for the development of children. In this study, 13% of the study participants (n=71) was observed to be orphan and unaware about their parents. Only 23% (n=127) had their single parent (either father or mother) and 64% children (n=356) was found to have their both parents alive (figure-10).

Figure-10: Parental status of street children (N=554)

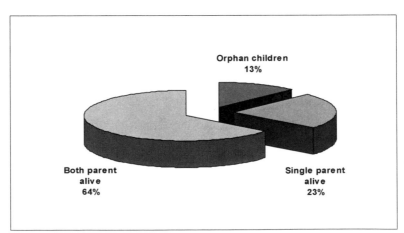

So far contact with family members was concerned, 36% children (n=197) reported that they didn't have any contact with their families, whereas 64% participants (n=357) stated to have contact with their family members, which was very irregular and infrequent (figure-11).

Figure-11:- Contact with families of street children (N=554)

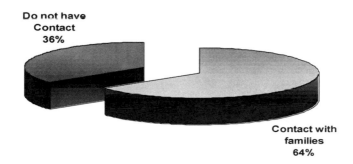

Since street is considered as home to the street children, 39% children (n=214) reported that they used to sleep under open air. About 61% of the study participants (n=340) were lucky to get some kind of shelter while sleeping at night. Of them, 13% (n=45) used to sleep under permanent shelter but most (87%; n=295) used to sleep under temporary shelter (figure-12).

Figure-12: Sleeping places of street children (n=340)

Though a group of children (39%) didn't get chance to sleep under shelter, but some of them managed either temporary or permanent shelter at night. Majority (85%; n=469) of them used to sleep under some public temporary shelter like railway platform, abandoned buildings, condemned railway compartments, vehicle parking places, under flyover etc. Only 15% participants (n=85) were reported to sleep under private temporary places that was usually linked with their jobs like small tea stalls, road-side dhabas or small hotels etc (figure-13).

Fig 13: Types of sleeping place of street children at night (N=554)

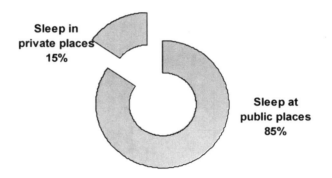

Personal Health & Hygiene

World Health Organization (WHO) defines, 'Health' is a state of complete physical, mental and social well-being and not merely the absence of disease and 'Hygiene' is the science that deals with the promotion and preservation of health. This study has highlighted oral hygiene, place of defecation and bathing habits as part of studying hygiene of street children.

Most children (80%; n=445) were said to wash their mouth regularly, whereas 20% participants (n=109) never did it. Of the children, who washed their mouth regularly, only 22% children (n=97) clean their mouth by brushing with paste. Ash was the commonest mode of mouth washing agent and was used by 51% participants (n=224). Other washing agents were plain water & tree stick and were used by 24% (n=109) & 3% children (n=15) respectively (figure-14).

38

Figure-14:- Maintenance of oral hygiene & mode of doing it (N=554)

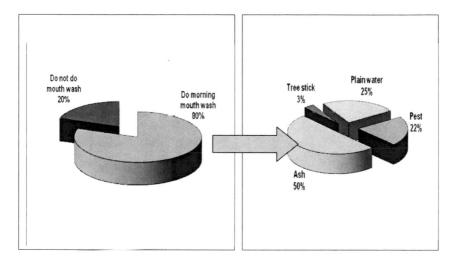

Place of defecation also play a vital role to know the status of hygiene and majority (71%) of them (n=393) were reported to defecate in open air that included periphery of ponds, both sides of railway tracks, discarded buildings etc. Only 29% of the participants (n=161) use toilets for defecation purpose (figure-15).

Figure-15:- Place of defecation of street children (N=554)

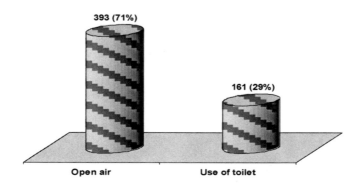

Hand washing following defecation appears to be a good practice. In this study it was observed that 18% study participants (n=101) never washed their hands after defecation where

39

as most (82%; n=453) were found to wash their hands with different cleaning agents following defecation. Of them, 51% children (n=232) washed their hands with plain

Figure-16:- Hand washing after defecation (N=554) & washing agent (n=453)

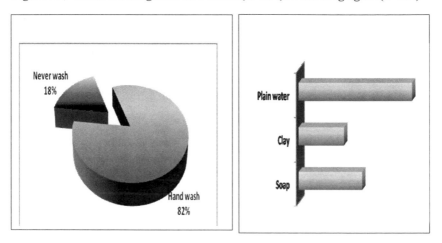

followed by washing with soap (29%; n=129) and mud (20%; n=92).

Regular bathing is also a major concern for good hygiene and most (61%) of the street children (n=340) were observed to take bath daily. Rest takes bath in variable frequency in a week as shown in figure-17. Only 1% children (n=8) didn't take bath even once in a week.

Figure-17:- Frequency of taking bath in a week (N=554)

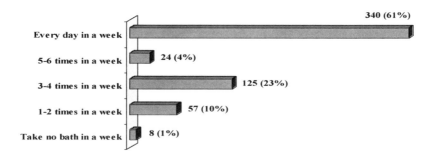

40

So far intake of regular meal is concerned, most (52%) of them (n=286) were found not taking even two major meals like lunch and dinner on regular basis. Only 48% children (n=268) were found to take both lunch and dinner regularly (figure-18).

Figure-18:- Street children taking two regular meals [lunch & dinner] (N=554)

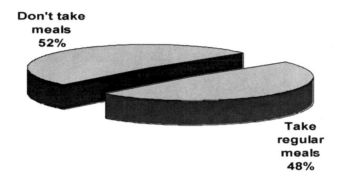

Don't take meals 52%

Take regular meals 48%

Of them who were unable to take two major meals, 61% children (n=174) reported that they couldn't take lunch & dinner due to lack of money. About 37% participants (n=107) reported that they were not allowed to take regular meals on time by their employers to avoid loss of continuity of work (like loading & unloading of a vehicle with goods). Only 1.7% of them (n=5) were found unwilling to take regular meals due to their addiction habit (figure-19).

Figure-19:- Response to why don't you take at least two regular meals? (n=286)

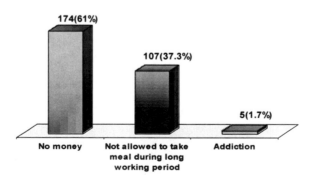

174(61%)

107(37.3%)

5(1.7%)

No money   Not allowed to take meal during long working period   Addiction

Majority of the study participants (90%; n=499) couldn't consume meal containing fish or egg or meat during last three days since the date of interview for this study. Only 10% of them (n=55) consumed either fish or egg or meat at least once during the said period (figure-20).

Figure-20: Consumption of fish/meat/egg during last three days (N=554)

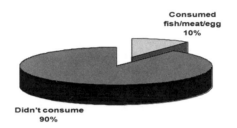

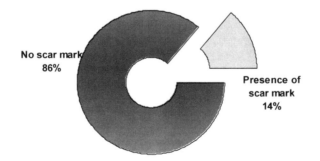

Regarding vaccination with BCG (evidenced by observing scar mark), 86% of the children (n=477) were found not vaccinated with BCG vaccine indicated by absence of BCG scar mark on their left upper arms. Only 14% (n=77) had the presence of scar marks suggestive of BCG vaccination (figure-21).

Figure-21: Immunization status indicated by scar mark of BCG (N=554)

Violence & Injury

Violence followed by physical assault is said to be a common phenomenon in street living children. In this study, 36% of the study participants (n=197) reported to have physical assaults on one or more occasions by the adult members of civil society within past one month. Of them, most (91%; n=179) were committed by the local police people. About 64% of the study participants (n=357) reported to have not faced any type of violence in their street life (figure-22).

Figure-22:- Physical assault faced by street children within last one month (N=554)

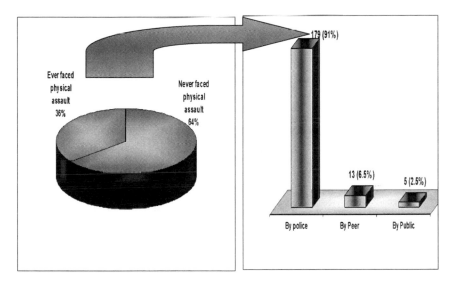

Conflict of street children among themselves for sharing of food, shelter or recreation is a common phenomenon in their street life. Sixteen percent of them (n=91) reported to face such types of conflicts where as 84% children (n=463) didn't report any type of conflict happened among them within past one month (figure-23).

43

Figure-23: Street children having conflicts within themselves for food, shelter (N=554)

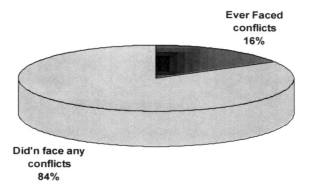

Ever Faced
conflicts
16%

Did'n face any
conflicts
84%

Street children due to their social circumstances may involve in criminal activities. About 8% of the studied children (n=42) were arrested by the police due to commitment of crimes within past 6 month (figure-24).

Figure-24:- Street children arrested within last six months due to crime (N=554)

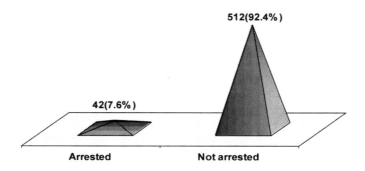

512(92.4%)

42(7.6%)

Arrested   Not arrested

Of the crimes committed by the study participants, majority was found to be associated with stealing (54.8%; n=23). This was followed by commitment of drug peddling that was

44

observed in 19% participants (n=8). About 26% participants (n=11) reported that they were arrested with false charges where actually they did not have any fault (figure-25).

Figure-25: Types of crime committed by street children (n=42)

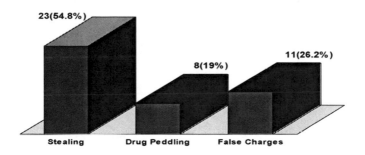

Civil society appears to be usually negative about street children and children's perspective is that they are often ignored by our society. In this study, 61% of the participants (n=339) felt that community was indifferent towards them. Twenty four percent of them (n=132) had a feeling of hatred by the society, 9% children (n=50) felt that they are somehow accepted by them and 6% of them (n=33) didn't have any idea about it. (Figure-26)

Figure-26:- Attitude of civil society towards street children (N=554)

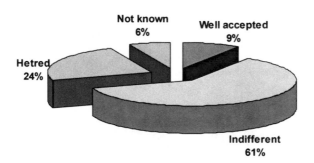

Non-tobacco Substance Abuse

Substance abuse, particularly smoking habits in young age is viewed as a common problem among street children. In this study, 22% studied children (n=122) reported that they were exclusive smokers and didn't experience substances other than 'Bidi' or 'cigarette' as shown in figure-27.

Figure-27:- Exclusive Smoking among street children (N=554)

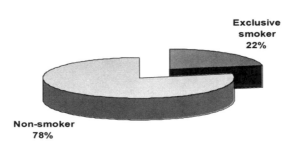

So far, non-tobacco substance abuse is concerned, 30% of them (n=165) was found to indulge various chemical substances whereas, 70% (n=389) didn't do so (figure-28).

Figure-28:- Intake of non-tobacco substances by street children (N=554)

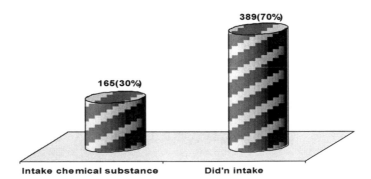

46

Age of initiation of non-tobacco substances in children is a matter of concern. In this study, majority of them (47.3%; n=78) was found to initiate it in the age of 11-15 year, followed by 6-10 years (42.4%; n=70), followed by 16 year & above age group (10%; n=17) [figure-29].

Figure-29:- Age of initiation of non-tobacco substance (n=165)

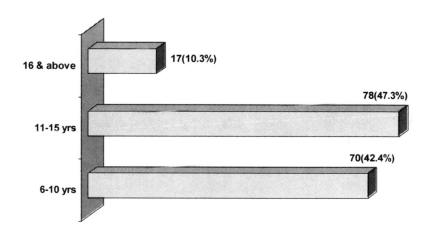

Overall prevalence of non-tobacco substance abuse was 29.4%. Figure-31 shows the observed age and sex-wise distribution of non-tobacco substance abuse pattern among study participants. The blue line represents the age-wise distribution of male subjects and the red line presents the same distribution of female subjects. It is evident from the figure that the rate of substance abuse is much higher in all age groups for males compared to that of females. It is also evident that the rate of non-tobacco substance abuse increases with age in males, whereas in females the rate remains almost the same in both 6 – 10 yrs and 15 yrs age group, after which it shows a sudden increase.

47

Figure-30: Age & sex-wise distribution of substance abuse in study participants (n=165)

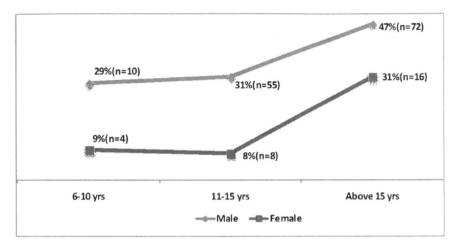

The commonest drug was 'Dendrite', an adhesive paste, that was consumed by 43% of the participants (n=104), followed by consumption of Ganja (25%; n=61), followed by consumption of Alcohol (16% (n=39). Other substances consumed by them were Brown Sugar (11%; n=27), Nitrazipum (2%; n=4), pure Heroin (3%; n=7) [figure-31].

Figure-31:- Non-tobacco substance abuse of the study participants (n=165)

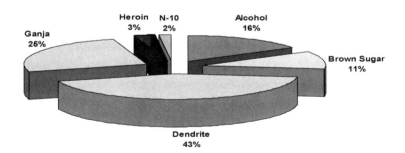

So far initiation of non-tobacco substance was concerned, majority of them (73%; n=121) was found to initiate this habit due to pressure from their peer group. Thirteen percent (n=21) used to initiate this out of curiosity, 8% (n=13) was found to take drugs due to depression and 6% (n=10) initiated this to over come their heavy work load (figure-32).

Figure-32:- Reason of initiating substance abuse by street children (n=165)

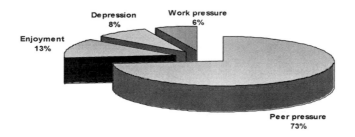

Regarding frequency of consumption of non-tobacco substance per day, 61.2% (n=101) consumed 1-2 times per day, followed by 26.7% (n=44) consumed 3-4 times per day followed by 8% (n=16) consumed 5-6 times per day followed by 1.8% (n=3) consumed it 7 – 8 times per day (figure-33)

Figure-33:- Frequency of consumption of non-tobacco substance/day (n=165)

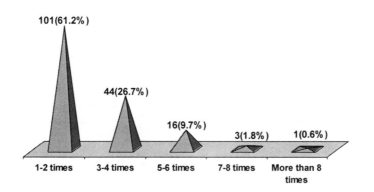

49

Daily expenditure for substance abuse revealed that most (52.7%; n=87) used to spend Rs.50/- to 100/- per day, followed by Rs.100/- to 150/- per day (4.8%; n=8), followed by Rs. 151/- to 200/- (3%; n=5) and only 2 participants used to spend more than Rs. 200/- per day for the consumption of non-tobacco substances (figure-34)

Figure-34:- Daily expenditure for consumption of non-tobacco substances (n=165)

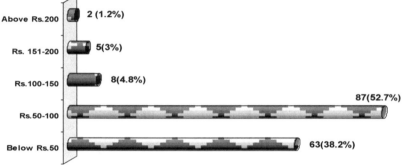

Regarding consistency of non-tobacco substances, it was observed that 94% of the abusers (n=155) used to abuse it regularly at least once a day. Only 6% of them (n=10) was found to consume it irregularly as shown in figure-35.

Figure-35:- Consistency of non-tobacco substances (n=165)

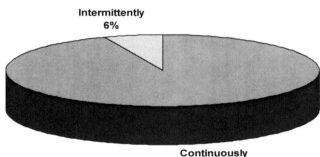

Majority of them (63%; n=104) was found to abuse substances with their peers. Twenty percent children (n=33) was found to abuse it absolutely alone and 17% did it either alone or in a group with peers (figure-36).

Figure-36: Substance abuse and number of partner/s with whom they share (n=165)

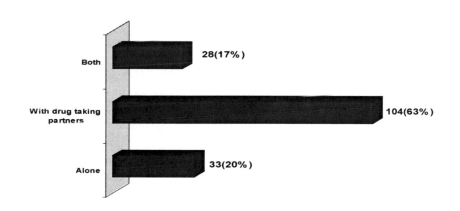

Regarding average number of substance abusing partners, majority of them (67%; n=89) had 1-5 partners, followed by 6-10 partners (23%; n=30), followed by 11-15 partners (3%). Street children also had more than 15 partners (7%) on an average during abuse (Figure-37).

Figure-37: Average number of drug taking partners of street children (n=132)

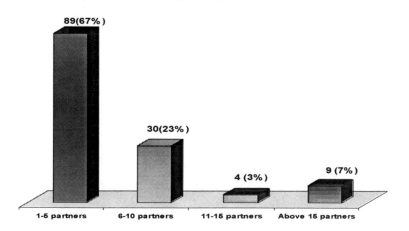

So far route of substance abuse was concerned, inhalation was the preferred route for most of them (70%; n=115). Oral route was preferred by 8% of participants (n=14) and 22% of them (n=36) used to consume it both by oral as well as inhalation (Figur-38).

Figure-38:- Preferred route of non-tobacco substance abuse (n=165)

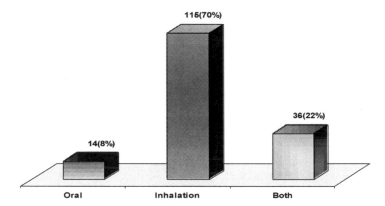

The participants were asked on how they could manage their substance addiction if they didn't have money to buy that. Majority of them (64.2%; n=106) was found be supported financially by their friends in need. This was followed by allowing them for sharing of drugs (16.4%; n=27) with their friends. About 9% abuser (n=14) reported that they didn't take drugs at that time. Some of them were supported by their families & few managed it by stealing and others did extra work to meet the cost of it as shown in figure-39.

Figure-39: Response to how do manage your substance abuse when you don't have money (n=165)

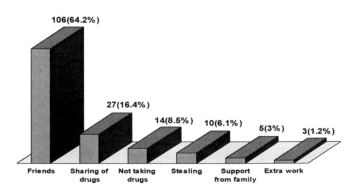

Sexual urge is known to either increase or decrease depending on the nature of non-tobacco substances. In this study, majority of them (57%; n=93) reported that sexual urge neither increase nor decrease following drug abuse. Twenty five percent of them (n=42) experienced an increased sexual urge after taking drugs, where as 18% abuser (n=30) didn't have any idea about sexual urge following substance abuse (figure-40).

Figure-40: Change of sexual urge following non-tobacco substance abuse (n=165)

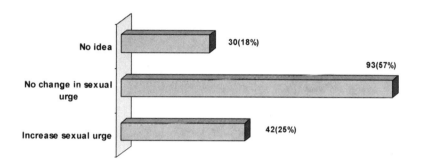

So far substance abuse related health problems were concerned, 33% (n=54) faced health problems related to substance abuse and 67% of them (n=111) didn't face such problems (figure-41).

Figure-41: Health problems due to substance abuse (n=165)

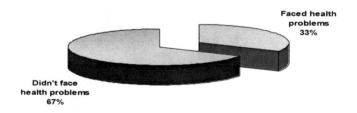

Health related problems caused by substance abuse in children are a major concern. In this study, withdrawal symptoms were faced by many of the abusers (30%; n=16). Of them, abdominal pain was the commonest (46%; n=15). Other features were insomnia, anorexia, vomiting and diarrhoea as shown in figure-42.

Figure-42: Types of health problems faced by study participants (n=54)

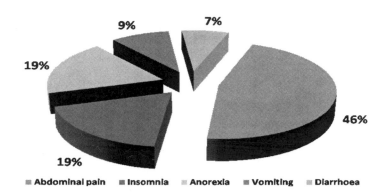

It is known to all that counseling service has a positive impact on substance abusers. Here, only one of the children (0.2%) reported to receive counseling against their substance abuse where as majority (99.8%; n=553) didn't receive it (Figure-43).

Figure-43: Response of street children receiving counseling services (N=554)

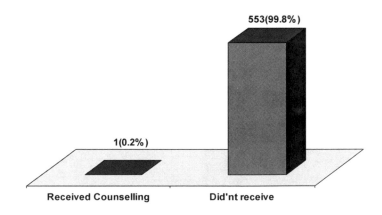

The types of substances consumed by male & female study subjects were many and shown in figure-44. Pink bar represents the male distribution and the green bar represents the female distribution of the consumed drugs. Overall, commonest drug was dendrite in both male & female children and specifically, pure heroin and brown sugar was not the drug of choice for female abusers (figure-44).

Figure-44:- Sex-wise distribution of types of substances consumed by study participants (n=165)

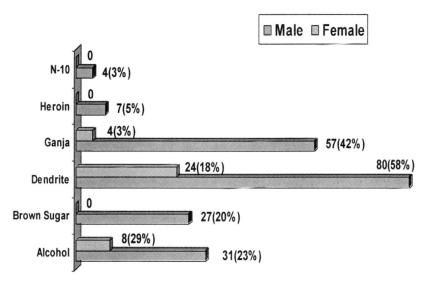

Table-4 shows some factors that are likely to be associated with substance abuse among street children. Age-wise, 11 year or older had substance abuse prevalence of 31.6% compared to the same of 22.5% in less than 11 year old children. This difference was found to be statistically significant on univariate analysis indicated by odds ratio (OR) of 2 and 95% confidence interval (CI) was 1 – 3.9. But this difference was not found to be significant on multivariate analysis. Male children had a substance abuse prevalence of 38% and the same was 15% in female children. This difference was statistically significant on both univariate as well as multivariate analysis indicated by OR = 3.5 & 2.3 and 95% CI = 2.2 – 5.8 & 1.4 – 4.1 respectively. Orphan children had a substance abuse prevalence of 43.3% where as substance abuse prevalence was 23.6% in children with parents. This difference was found to be statiscally significant

Table-4:-Risk factors for Substance abuse with odds ratio & confidence interval at 95% level

Factors	Total No.	No. of substance Abuser	Odds Ratio(CI at 95% level)	
			Univariate	Multivariate
Age of 11 year or more	478	151 (31.6%)	2 (1 – 3.9)	Not significant
Age of 10 year or less	76	14 (22.5%)		
Male	362	137 (38%)	3.5 (2.2 – 5.8)	2.3 (1.4 – 4.1)
Female	192	28 (15%)		
Orphan children	173	75 (43.3%)	2.4 (1.6 – 3.6)	Not significant
Children having parents	381	90 (23.6%)		
Children having no contact with families	197	99 (50.2%)	4.4 (2.9 – 6.6)	Not significant
Children having contact with families	357	66 (18.4%)		
Night stay in public places	469	156 (33.2%)	4.2 (1.9 – 9.2)	5.4 (2.4 – 12.5)
Night stay in private places	85	9 (10.5%)		

taking no bath since last 7 days and irregular/ infrequent food intake among substance only on univariate analysis indicated by OR = 2.4 & 95% CI = 1.6 – 3.6. Similarly, children having no contact with family had higher substance abuse prevalence of 50.2% compared to children having family contact (18.4%). This difference has statistical significance on univariate analysis indicated by OR of 4.4 and 95% CI = 2.9 – 6.6 but not significant on multivariate analysis. Considering night stay of street children at public places, substance abuse prevalence (33.2%) had higher compared to their counterparts (10.5%) and this difference was found to be statistically significant on univariate analysis (OR= 4.2; 95% CI = 1.9 – 9.2) as well as multivariate analysis (OR = 5.4; 95% CI = 2.4 – 12.5) also, as shown in table-4. So, factors like older age of 11 year or more, male children, orphan children, children having no contact with families and night stay in public places might be considered as risk factors for substance abuse in this study.

Table-5 has presented the effects of substance abuse on violence, hygiene, sexual abuse, criminal offence, food intake etc. Violence committed on substance abusers was found to be 54% compared to the same of 28% among substance non-users. This difference was statistically significant (Odds Ratio = 3; 95% CI = 2 – 4.5). Sexual abuse committed on substance abusers was found to be 13.3% compared to the same of 7.4% in non-users. This difference was also statistically significant indicated by OR = 1.9 and 95% CI = 1 - 3.5. Prevalence of crime followed by police arrest among substance abusers was found to be 23.6% and the same of non-substance abuser was 5.1%. This difference was statistically significant (OR = 5.7 & CI = 3 – 10.5). Poor oral hygiene among substance abusers was 35.7% and the same of non- substance abuser was 12.8%. This difference was statistically significant indicated by OR = 3.7 & 95% CI = 2.4 – 5.9. Prevalence of no bath since last 7 days among substance users was 61.2% and the same of non-abusers was 29%. This difference was also statistically significant (OR = 3.8 & 95% CI = 2.5 – 5.7). Irregular or infrequent food intake among substance abusers was found to be 66.6% and it was 45.2% among non- substance abusers. This difference was statistically significant indicated by OR = 2.4 and 95% CI = 1.6 – 3.6. Violence committed on substance abusers, sexual abuse committed on substance abusers, crime followed by police arrests among substance abuser, poor oral hygiene among substance abusers, abusers, all these were the effects of substance abuse.

Table- 5:- Effect of Substance abuse on violence, hygiene, sexual abuse, crime and Food intake with odds ratio and level of significance

Factors	Total No.	No. of substance Abuser	Odds Ratio	Confidence Interval at 95% level
Violence committed on substance abusers	165	89 (54%)		
Violence committed on non-abusers	389	108 (28%)	3	2 – 4.5
Sexual abuse committed on substance Users	165	22 (13.3%)	1.9	1 – 3.5
Sexual abuse committed on non-users	389	29 (7.4%)		
Crime followed by police arrest among subs. Abusers	165	39 (23.6%)		
Crime followed by police arrest among non-substance abusers	389	20 (5.1%)	5.7	3 – 10.5
Poor Oral hygiene among substance Abuser	165	59 (35.7%)		
Poor Oral hygiene among non-substance Abuser	389	50 (12.8)	3.7	2.4 – 5.9
No bath since last 7days among abusers	165	101 (61.2%)		
No bath since last7 days among non-abuser	389	113 (29%)	3.8	2.5 – 5.7
Irregular/ infrequent food intake among abusers	165	110 (66.6%)		
Regular food intake among non-abusers	389	176 (45.2%)	2.4	1.6 – 3.6

Sexual Abuse

So far sexual abuse is concerned, overall prevalence of sexual abuse was found to be 9% (n=51) among studied street children. Age-wise, highest prevalence was observed in age group of 11-15 year (39%; n=20), followed by 6-10 year age-group (31%; n=16), followed by age group of 15 years and above (29%; n=15), as shown in figure-45.

Figure-45: Age-wise distribution of sexual abuse in street children (n=51)

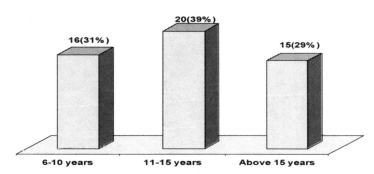

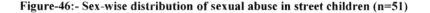

Sex-wise, male children had a higher sexual abuse prevalence (65%; n=33) compared to the same of female (35%; n=18) as evident from the figure-46.

Figure-46:- Sex-wise distribution of sexual abuse in street children (n=51)

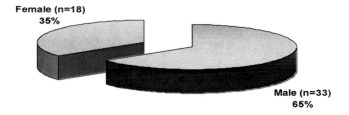

Sexual abuse appears to be higher among male children compared to female up to the age of 15 year. But female children have a higher sexual abuse than male counterpart in above 15 yr. age group [figure-47]. This figure shows, as age increases sexual abuse decreases in males.

59

But in case of female, it shows a decreasing trend till 15 year of age (from 17% to 4%) after which it sharply increases from 4% to 13% at the age of above 15 year.

Figure-47: Age & sex-wise distribution of sexual abuse in study participants (n=51)

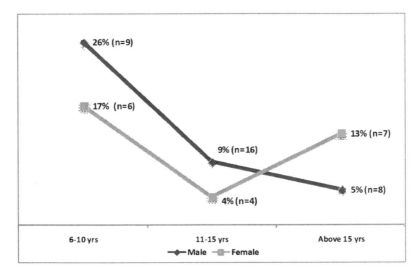

So far age of first sexual abuse is concerned, commonest age group was observed to be 6-10 year age group (49%; n=25), this was followed by age group of 11-15 year (39.2%; n=20), followed by above 15 years (11.8%; n= 6) as shown in figure-48.

Figure-48: Age of first sexual abuse in street children (n=51)

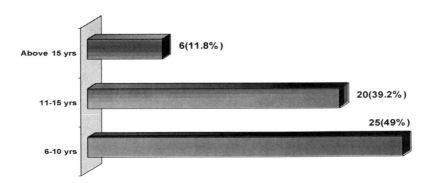

60

Figure-49 shows about nature of sexual abusing events committed on studied participants. Common abusing events were hugging by same as well as opposite sex (69%; n= 35), kissing (33%; n= 17) by both sexes, attempted for sex (65%; n= 33), forceful exposure of genitalia (61%; n= 31) to the abuser & forceful touching of genitalia (18%; n= 9) of the subject as shown in figure-49. From the figure, it is evident that forceful penetrative sex was committed on 12 (23%) male children whereas no female children reported that type of abuse in this study.

Figure-49: Sex-wise distribution of nature of sexual abuse in study participants (n=51)

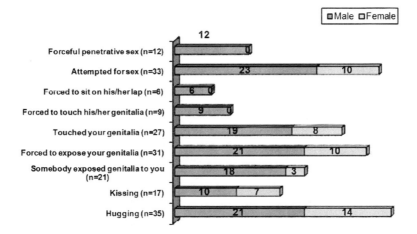

Regarding sexual abuser of street children, more than half of the participants (53%; n=27) were abused by single person on single occasion. Twenty seven percent (n=14) of them were abused by single person but on multiple occasions where as only 20% of them (n=10) abused on multiple occasions by multiple persons as shown in figure-50.

Figure-50: Sexual abuser of street children (n=51)

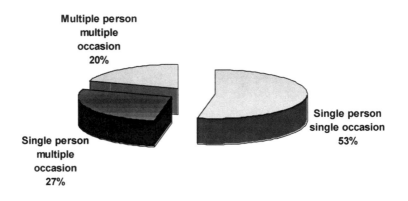

Table-6 shows some factors that are likely to be associated with sexual abuse among street children. Age-wise, 10 year or less had sexual abuse prevalence of 21% compared to the same of 7.2% among children in age of 11 year or more. This difference was found to be statistically significant in univariate analysis indicated by odds ratio of 3.3 and 95% CI of 1.6 – 6.7. This difference was statistically significant on multivariate analysis also by indicating OR of 2.8 and 95% CI was 1.3 – 5.8. Orphan children had sexual abuse prevalence of 27.6% and the same was 8.2% in children with parents. This difference was statistically significant (OR = 4.2; 95% CI = 1.6 – 10) on univariate analysis but it was not significant on multivariate analysis. Similarly, prevalence of sexual abuse among children having no contact with family was found to be 16%, whereas the same was 5% among children having family contact. This difference has statistical significance on univariate analysis indicated by OR = 3.4 and 95% CI = 1.8 – 6.5 but found to be not significant on multivariate analysis. Spending night at public places had a higher sexual abuse prevalence of 10% compared to their counterparts (2.4%) and this difference was statistically significant (OR = 4.8 & 95% CI = 1.2 – 4.1) on univariate analysis but this was not significant on multivariate analysis as shown in table-6. So, factors like younger age of 10 year or less, orphan children, children having no contact with families and night stay in public places might be considered as risk factors for sexual abuse in this study.

Table- 6: Risk factors for Sexual abuse with odds ratio and level of significance

Factors	Total No.	No. of sexual Abuser	Odds Ratio (CI at 95% level)	
			Univariate	Multivariate
Age of 10 years or less	76	16 (21%)		
Age of 11 year or more	478	35 (7.3%)	3.3 (1.6 – 6.7)	2.8 (1.3 – 5.8)
Orphan children	29	8(27.6%)		
Children having parents	525	43(8.2%)	4.2 (1.6 - 10)	Not significant
Children having no contact with family	197	32(16%)		
Children having contact with family	357	19(5%)	3.4 (1.8 – 6.5)	Not significant
Night stay in public place	469	49(10%)		
Night stay in private place	85	2(2.4%)	4.8 (1.2 – 4.1)	Not Significant

Table-7 has presented the effects of sexual abuse on violence and substance abuse. Violence during sexual abuse was found to be 53% compared to the same of 34% among non abuser. This difference was statistically significant (OR=2.2; 95% CI= 1.2 – 4). Substance abuse was 43% among sexually abused children where as it was 28% in non-abused children. This difference was also statistically significant indicated by OR = 1.9 and 95% CI = 1- 3.5. That means substance abuse and violence had certain effects on sexual abuse.

Table- 7: Relationship between sexual abuse and violence & substance abuse

Factors	Total No.	No. of substance Abuser	Odds Ratio	Confidence Interval at 95% level
Violence committed on sexually abused children iolence on non-abused	51 503	27 (53%) 170 (34%)	2.2	1.2 – 4
Substance abuser children facing sexual abuse Non-substance abuser children facing sexual abuse	51 503	22 (43%) 143 (28%)	1.9	1 – 3.5

Sexual Practices

Though sexual practices are not common among children of that age, but 35% children (n=194) reported to have physical relationship with opposite sex as well as same sex partners, where as 65% children (n=360) didn't have any physical relationship as shown in figure-51.

Figure-51: Reported sexual practices of studied street children (N=554)

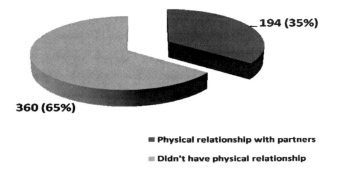

194 (35%)

360 (65%)

■ Physical relationship with partners

▨ Didn't have physical relationship

Regarding visiting sex workers, 13% of studied male children (n=47) reported to visit sex workers within last one month, where as 87% children (n=315) never visited sex workers as shown in figure-52.

Figure-52: Visiting sex workers by the male children within last one months (n=362)

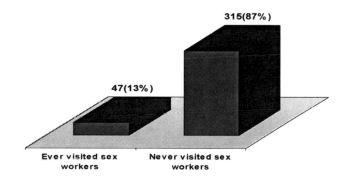

Regarding suffering from sexually transmitted infections (STIs), most of the study participants (87%; n=481) reported that they didn't suffer from any sexually transmitted infection. Only 13% of them (n=73) reported to suffer from STIs within last six months as shown in figure-53. Of them, majority (88%; n= 27) had problem of discharge from their genital organs as clinical symptom (figure-53). About 28% participants (n=20) had a symptom of ulcer and 34% (n=24) had symptoms of both ulcer and discharge as reported by physician.

Figure-53: Reported sexually transmitted infections in children (N=554) & symptoms

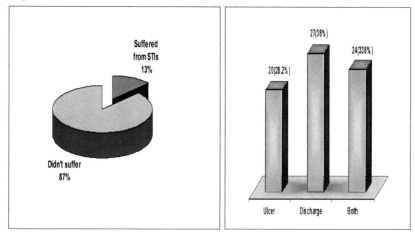

Regarding knowledge about HIV/AIDS, 53% (n=291) heard about HIV/AIDS where as 47% (n=263) never heard about it (figure-54).

Figure-54: Heard about HIV/AIDS (N=554)

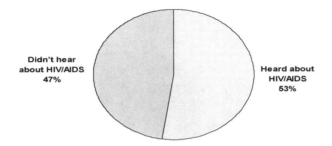

Regarding knowledge on HIV transmission, 55% (n=159) didn't have any knowledge on HIV transmission. About 40% (n=115) children knew that unsafe sexual practice was one of the routes of HIV transmission, followed by contaminated needle / syringe (3%; n=10), followed by through unsafe blood transfusion (2.4%; n=7) [figure-55].

Figure-55: Knowledge about HIV Transmission (n=291)

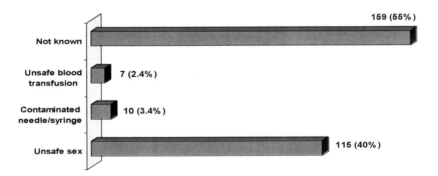

HIV, HBV and VDRL sero-positivity of the study subjects revealed that the overall HIV ser-prevalence was 1% (n=6), that of Hepatitis-B was 6% (n=35) and the same of VDRL was 4% (n=22) among these studied children. (figure-56).

Figure-56: Sex-wise HIV, HBV & VDRL Sero-positivity (N=554)

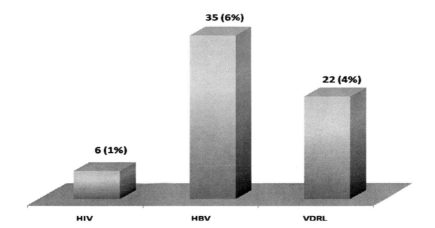

67

DISCUSSION

Over the past three decades both developed as well as developing countries face the problem of street children and the numbers of which appear to be rising day by day (Black,1993). The increase in number of street children is primarily caused by broken families, single parenthood, abusive, neglectful, immoral and irresponsible parents but the major underlying cause is extreme poverty.

In this study a total of 554 street children were interviewed. Age-wise, almost half of them (49.5%; n=274) was in the age group of 11-15 years followed by above 15 year age group (36.8%; n=204), followed by 6 -10 year (23%; n=74) with a median age of 13 year. A similar observation was observed in Nepal where commonest age group of street children was 10-14 year (63%) followed by 15-17 year (29%) with a median age of 13 year (Subedi,G, 2002). Studies of street children in poor third world countries differ from rich first world countries. Here street children were in the age group of 11 – 16 year or above 16 year (Richter,1991). Other study in Pakistan observed that 96% was male children with a median age of 13 years (Sherman & Plitt, 2005). Studies in Nigeria, Columbia, Ethiopia and Afghanistan Showed that the age of street children were ranging from 9 - 12 year (Aderinto, 2000); (Lalor, 1999); (Senanayake, Ranasinghe, & & Balasuriya, 1994); (Benalcazar, 1982); (Terredes, 2002); (Aptekar, 1988). Similar study in Brazil also documented, median age of 14 year among study participants (Fernanda, Neiva, & Ramos, 2006). This indicates that the street children of South-east Asian countries face similar problems particularly the time when they get out of their families and choose street life. A study on street children in Pretoria, South Africa, also found similar findings indicating an average age of South African street children was approximately 13 year (Le, 1996). This could be due to the fact that most of these children had to struggle against severe poverty and to stay away from this hardship and they are pushed to cities for the searching of any job at this early age.

Gender-wise 65% male and 35% female children were participated in this study. This male predominance among street children may not be the reality as observed in this study. Similar cross-sectional study was conducted among street children of Brazil where males were proportionately higher (66%) compared to females (30%) children (Fernanda, Neiva, & Ramos, 2006). Considering all the social factors, poor families (mainly single parent household) push their male children to go forward for earning in order to supplement family income and train female children to take over all the household responsibilities. At the initial phase, girl children were engaged either in household job or worked as maidservant in their locality. But boys didn't hesitate to go out for searching job where they found any possibility. For that reason male population was predominant in studies of different countries. This picture was also reflected in the present study. A study in Pakistan also found the preponderance of male (81%) children compared to females (19%) on the street (Moazzam, Saqib, & Hiroshi, 2004). Similar finding was observed from South African study, where 104 male and 39 female populations were studied (Le, 1996). Many studies from different parts of the country also documented that majority of the children on the street was males (Polat, 2009), (UNICEF, 2009); (Moazzam, Saqib, & Hiroshi, 2004); (Baybuga, 2002), (Hadi, 2000). Though studies from Asia, Latin America and Africa report the predominance of male children (Terredes, 2002); (Aderinto, 2000); (Beyene & Berhane, 1997); (Black & Farrington, 1997); (Wright & Karnisky, 1993) but most of the studies in USA documented uniform gender distribution among street children (Farrow, Deisher, & Brown, 1992).

Though primary education is an essential requirement for children, but many of them are deprived of that due to extreme poverty. Among all the participants, 40% children (n=221) had some kind of formal education, and 13% (n=75) had non-formal education where as 47% (n=258) children were found to have neither formal nor non-formal education, that means they were totally illiterate. It was reported that out of 221 study participants, some children used to go to school at their early ages but they couldn't continue their study for long period due to financial constraints in their family. Some children dropped out from school due to the death of their parents, others discontinued their study because they were forced to run away from home. Although most of them reported to like to go back to their school lives in order to secure a better future, but spending longer time on the street didn't allow them to do so for educational rehabilitation. A similar finding was noticed in a study in Pakistan where almost all participants left school or couldn't continue it due to poverty (Moazzam, Saqib, & Hiroshi, 2004). Study participants, who had formal education, were not willing to take the opportunity of some kind of informal education offered by the local NGOs or related agencies with the aim of improving their basic education including children who do not have any type of education at all. A study in Brazil has found that 25% children lived with their parents & went to school where as 46% participants used to live with their families but didn't go to school (Forster LM, 1996).

So far marital status was concerned, 95% (n=342) male children and 67% female children (n=128) were found to be never married in this study. It was also observed that average age of

70

study participants was 13 year and among them, 4% of the male (n=16) and 30% of the female participants (n=58) were married and living together. That means, early marriage is prevalent among these children; especially female children were married at their very early ages. Most of the female children were married within the age of 10- 15 year. Ideally, this should not the minimum age of marriage in any country including India, because of its multi-faceted consequences like poor maternal & child health, chronic ill health, anaemia, malnutrition etc.. Big size of the family leading to poverty has been identified as one of the important causes of early marriage of female children. Generally, female children are considered as economic burden to their poor parents. This probably leads their parents to go for early marriage of their daughters to save the life of other members of the family. Among female participants, 3% of them (n=6) was observed as married but separated from their husband, where as only 1% male participant (n=4) was reported to be separated from their wives. It was a major finding that the rate of separation after marriage was also higher in female children. The most common reason of separation for female may be due to their young age, illiteracy, inadequate knowledge about sexual life, lack of empowerment, ignorance of women's right etc. Due to all these factors, female children are deprived easily by the society.

Children get out of their families where adequate family support is not available or totally non-existent. In search of better lives & survival, children usually migrate from their house or adjoining areas to more developed areas where job facilities appear to be better. Migration usually occurs from rural to urban areas and from small cities to bigger cities. After migrated from rural areas, children are clustered in the areas close to the railway stations and market places where job opportunities are said to be better. Though this is not the actual age to engage in any type of work, but this study has documented that most (72%) of the children (n=398) were engaged in different types of work at this early age (including health hazardous jobs), to support themselves and or families. Only 28% of them (n=156) were remained jobless at the time of this study. A study among street children in South Africa has documented that severe poverty is a typical precondition of a child's early entry into employment (De, 1998); (Black M. , 1993). This has also been confirmed by studies in Brazil (Aneci, Borba, & & Ebrahim, 1992), Columbia (Aptekar, 1988), Ethiopia (Lalor, 1999), and Nigeria (Aderinto, 2000).

Among the working children, 32% of them (n=128) had worked for themselves as they had no other financial support. Rest (68%; n=270) were engaged in different types of work to support themselves as well as their family members. Some were orphan, who worked for their daily bread & butter. Most of the study participants (37.4%; n=149) were found to engage themselves in different types of small shops or hotels where they worked as a daily labor or helper. Other jobs done by them were rag picking (19%; n=115), van pulling (16%; n=64) etc. About 6% of them (n=21) were engaged in begging in market places or tourist spots and showing different games in trains or buses (1.2%; n=5) etc. It was also observed that a sizable number of children (5.8%; n=23) were engaged with dressing and packaging of fishes by their employers, mostly for exporting to some other places. Only 1 child was found to be involved in drug peddling. A section of working study participants was often allured to petty crimes (7.3%; n=29) like black-marketing, pick-pocketing etc. Children with criminal activity are probably caused by lack of parental guidance, loneliness, street life, long starvation etc. These factors along with peer influence slowly take them towards the dark-side of the life as mentioned above. Though this is not the age for children to work but reality is far from that is supposed to be. It was observed that a number of children were recruited on contract basis in small hotels & restaurants as dish washer, table attendant, helper in cooking etc and most common and shocking matter was that they were not paid a single paisa by their employer. They were compelled to shed their sweat day & night in exchange of two meals per day and a temporary shelter at night. In order to gain livelihoods, some children were forced to work in an exploitative situation just to fulfill their daily minimum needs. Some children aged 6-9 years were found to do work against their will by the instruction of older children like rag picking and empty water bottle collecting from the streets. The said working children have no right for selling these collected items directly to the retailers for recycling. In contrast, they were bound to hand over all these items to older children (who instructed to do so) and in return younger children were paid a nominal amount of commission on the basis of number of collecting items. A study in Pakistan also revealed that 36% of the study participants felt exploited and over-worked and 13% children complained about poor payment by their employer (Moazzam, Saqib, & Hiroshi, 2004). Another study in Kathmandu, Nepal, also explored that street children were engaged in various labour sectors. Rag picking was one of the most health hazardous jobs for these children and majority (36.4%) of them worked as rag pickers, collecting and selling plastic & metal scraps at the junkyards. Many children (26.3%) were dependent on begging in market or tourist places. 17.8% of them worked as conductor in small vehicle or buses while 42.4% children worked as porter in different market places (Rai & Ghimire, 2002).

Job period may be continuous or intermittent. About 52% of them (n=148) remained jobless up to 7 days and about 41% children (n=117) remained without job for 8-14 days, where as 5.3% participants (n=15) were jobless for more than 15 days in the previous month. Only 3 of them reported that they remained jobless for more than 21 days. When they become jobless, either begging or taking leftover/discarded food to meet their hunger is the option. If that does not satisfy their hunger even by above means, forced starvation is the only outcome to many of them. In this study, many jobless children used to receive their financial support from their peer group and family members (94%). Another study also documented that peers have an important place in the life of street children. Most of the children rely on their peer group because they are supported at the time of shortfalls (Rohde, Ferreira, Zomer, & Forster, 1998). In this study, 94% children (n=146) reported to maintain their livelihood with the help of their peers and family members. A small section of them (6%) were reported to get support by local Non-Governmental Organizations (NGOs). These NGOs were functional in local areas where street children were found in a good number. Generally these NGOs regularly offer two major meals and medical support for minor illnesses.

Majority (36%) of the children (n=145) earned Indian rupees of 501 to Rs.1000 per month. About 2% participant (n=7) had highest monthly income of above Rs.5000 and 7% was in the lowest income level of Rs.500 or less. Children who were engaged in stealing or pic-pocketing, income-wise they were in the highest income level of above Rs.5000 per month. Street children in Pakistan reported that they had to work for 8-12 hours daily with a nominal earning of 60 rupees daily (Moazzam, Saqib, & Hiroshi, 2004).

It is the traditional perspective that care, protection and upbringing of children should be the duty of their parents. But the present study observed that 13% children (n=71) were orphan and unaware of the status of their parents. These children reported that they had never seen their parents and did not know how they were moved towards that street life. Living alone on the street was definitely a big challenge for young as well as old children. About 23% (n=127) had their single parent either mother or father alive and 64% of them (n=356) was found to have their both parents alive. So without proper parental guidance, it is difficult to socialize them as well as prevent them from antisocial and improper behaviour. A study in Nepal observed similar findings of 71% child had their father alive where as 57% had only their mother (Subedi, 2002). Another study from Pakistan revealed that 88% of the children had only father alive and 87% had only mother and living with them (Moazzam, Saqib, & Hiroshi, 2004).

So far contact with family members is concerned, 36% (n=197) reported that they didn't have any contact with their families at all. That may be either they were orphan or they used to stay on the street due to the death of their parents. A study in Brazil has documented that most (71%) of the children always lived with their parents where as only 29% used to sleep on the street and they didn't have any contact with their families (Froster LM, 1996). Another study in Pakistan found majority (82%) of the children lived on the street with their parents, whereas 6.5% of them used to sleep independently and rests lived with their near relatives (Moazzam, Saqib, & Hiroshi, 2004). Some children had negative reaction about their families. They reported that after death of their parents, other members of their family forced them to leave home and snatched their property. Others reported that due to the habit of taking substances they used to sell household goods and stole money from family members that's why their families throw them away from their life and presently they live alone on the street and seek a sense of companionship with their peers. About 64% children (n=357) stated to have contact with their family members, which was very irregular and infrequent. Because, some of them consider themselves as a part of that family but have chosen the street as the place of their daytime activities. A number of children had to give total financial support to families from their nominal earning. So, they didn't want to spend much for their frequent visit to family. These children also have the habit of substance abuse and they realized that their parents might not take it easy, for that reason they do not like to maintain regular contact with their parents. They used to maintain contact with families but visit home occasionally. A study from South Africa estimated that about 33% of street children return home shortly, and another 33% stayed on the streets for more than 6-18 months. Most of the street children in developed countries return home within a month (Le, 1996).

As they had chosen street for their shelter, majority (85%; n=469) used to sleep at some public places like railway platform, abandoned buildings, condemned railway compartments, vehicle-parking places, under flyover, railway car-shed, under-construction buildings, beside garbage vat etc. Most of them reported that they were migrated from rural areas and had no other options than to live in the 'JHUPRIS' raised by them on the pavements, sides of railway tracks, on the bank of the water bodies, under fly-over, in the alleys adjacent to the parks & markets and other open public places in & around the city. Only 15% of them (n=85) reported

74

to sleep at private places that were usually at their job site like small tea stalls, road-side dhabas or small hotels. In exchange of their labour they were permitted to sleep. Out of 340 participants (61%), 13% (n=45) used to sleep under permanent shelter but most (87%; n=295) of them used to sleep under temporary shelter. About 39% of them (n=214), didn't have any shelter and used to sleep under open air.

Personal Health & Hygiene:

World Health Organization (WHO) defines, 'Health' is a state of complete physical, mental and social well-being and not merely the absence of disease and 'Hygiene' is the science that deals with the promotion and preservation of health. But all over the world, most street children do not enjoy basic needs such as health, education, nutrition and recreation. They to a large extent live in an unhygienic and polluted atmosphere. Their working and living environment puts a lot of strain on their physical as well as mental conditions. Malnourishment and other diseases are common in them.

So far oral hygiene is concerned, 80% children (n=445) were said to wash their mouth regularly, whereas 20% (n=109) didn't maintain it. Of the children, who washed their mouth regularly, only 22% (n=97) clean their mouth using paste. Ash was the commonest mode of mouth washing agent for them and was used by 51% study participants (n=224). Other washing agents were plain water & tree stick and were used by 24% (n=109) & 3% (n=15) respectively. It was observed that children living with their families (with both parents working), used paste for cleaning up their mouth. Children working in hotels were found to use ash that was the end-product of coal, for cleaning up their teeth. Generally, orphan children and children below 10 years of age, were not aware of oral hygiene and didn't have the habit of mouth washing. This may be due to the fact that the sense of hygiene was not developed among these children that require attention for intervention towards this.

Defecation habit of street children is a matter of great concern. Most studied children (71%; n=393) reported to defecate in open air that included periphery of ponds, both sides of railway tracks, discarded buildings etc. Generally, they were forced to do so as many of them couldn't afford to pay for toilet (available in railway platforms & market areas) regularly. Only 29% (n=161) was reported to use toilets for defecation. A study in Pakistan highlighted that only 33% children were able to access toilet and bathing facilities on the street (Moazzam, Saqib,

& Hiroshi, 2004). Generally they used platform toilet, toilet of train compartments, Government hospitals, public toilets etc. Hand washing following defecation appears to be a good practice but it was known that 18% participants (n=101) never washed their hands following defecation, whereas most (82%; n=453) were found to wash their hands with different cleaning agents. Of them, 51% children (n=232) washed their hands with plain water. Children who reported to defecate in toilet, usually washed their hands properly with soap (29%; n=129) either provided from pay toilet or by themselves. Participants defecating in public places were reported to use mud for hand washing following defecation. In this study, 61% of the participants (n=340) were found to take bath daily. Only 1% (n=8) didn't take bath even once in a week.

Intake of at least two regular meals is the basic needs of any human being. Growing children require it more for their growth & development. In this study, majority of them [52%; n=286] were found not taking two major meals like lunch and dinner on regular basis. Only 48% children (n=268) was found to take both lunch and dinner regularly. Among children, who were unable to take two major meals, 61% of them (n=174) couldn't arrange due to lack of money. About 37% children (n=107) reported that they were not allowed to take regular meals on time by their employers to avoid loss of continuity of work while doing their jobs at meal time. (like loading & unloading of a vehicle with goods). Similar findings were also documented in a study in Pakistan where only 63% children were able to get two major meals and 10% of them reported very irregular meal pattern (Moazzam, Saqib, & Hiroshi, 2004). Generally some of the children were engaged in loading and/or un-loading of goods on contract basis and payment was dependent on the complete loading or un-loading of a goods vehicle. Without completion of work, payment is withheld that forces children to work continuously with food. There are few non-governmental organizations that sometimes provide food to a limited number of street children. Some manage with left-over food from hotels, restaurants that are thrown on the street or in dustbin. Only 1.7% of them (n=5) were found unwilling to take regular meals due to their addiction habit.

So far intake of consumption of fish / egg / meat was concerned, 90% children (n=499) were found not consumed the above meal within last three days from the date of study (interview). Only 10% participants (n=55) who had contacts with their families at least once in a week, consumed fish / egg / meat once in a day (lunch or dinner). But children living without their families could not even think of fish / egg / meat in their daily meals because they had to struggle for avoiding daily hunger.

The protective role of immunization is very important for every child. Like other children, street children are equally or more vulnerable to vaccine preventable diseases. It was observed that 86% study children (n=477) did not receive BCG vaccination indicated by absence of BCG scar mark over upper half of left deltoid. Some of them reported that they were born on the street and never went to any hospital for any health related problems. Among all the study participants, only 14% children (n=77) who were born in local hospital or health centers had scar mark of BCG vaccination. This probably indicates non-receipt of other contemporary vaccines by many of them. This must be taken care of by the local health authority.

Violence & Injury:

Violence is the intentional use of physical force or power against oneself or others that results in injury, death, psychological harm, mal-development or deprivation.

Violence is a common crisis experienced by street children from an early age. This fundamentally affects children's development but is rarely focused by the government and other service providers like Non-Governmental Organizations (NGOs), Community Based Organizations (CBOs), Orphanage & Rescue Homes etc. Other than police & civil society members, street children are often tortured (snatch forcefully money and food) by their elder as well as physically strong peers and many others with whom they need to interact in day to day street life. Sometimes children are beaten up for unjustified reasons, ridiculed, traumatized and blamed easily since they have none to protect against violence.

Violence followed by physical assault is said to be a common phenomenon in street living children. These children are usually victims of violence, exploitation and abuses. The present study has documented that 36% of the study participants (n=197) faced physical assaults on one or more occasions by the adult members of civil society within past one month (w.e.f. date of interview). Majority of them (91%; n=179) were tortured by the local police people. Children are already living in marginalized situations and are extremely vulnerable and have less potential to protect themselves from abuse and violence. Police harassment was a great trouble-maker in the lives of street living children (Parker, 2002). Research from Africa, Latin

77

America and North America reported that violence by police (Agnelli, 1986); (White, 2002); (Harris, 2002) and sexual exploitation (Noell & & Ochs, 2001); (Lalor, 1999) made the life of street children a great suffering. Rarely police did a positive image to them. Children portrayed the police as an enemy, a fearful figure and one of the most distressing street experiences (Riberio, 2008). According to the children, police violence occurred in different ways: either they put an effort to remove the children from the streets against their will or they intended deliberately to humiliate them with verbal or physical aggression or kept them in police custody with false charges where they didn't have any fault. They also deliberately feel that police people viewed them as threat to contentment of society and misjudge them as thieves. Most of the time, they had to bite the bullet of bad experience as beaten-up, verbal abuse and arrest for vague offences. Most of the study participants reported that they were assaulted physically by police due to their vagabond nature, for moving here and there, resting at public places and due to taking substances on the open places. Children also confessed that some of them (8%; n=42) really committed criminal offences followed by police arrest in near past. Among them, 54.8% children (n=23) were associated with stealing and 19% of them (n=8) was engaged in drug peddling. Few (16%; n-91) of them were found to have conflict among themselves for sharing of food, shelter or recreation. Most of them managed their foodstuff by begging, from thrown away food of hotels or train passengers etc. About 26% participant (n=11) reported to be charged with false cases. All these depressing factors placed them in a corner. But considering all cases, the ultimate judgment of street children was that the main conflict with police and other people was due to the fact that they were minor, unsupervised and unprotected unlike other children.

Drugs and crime cannot be separated from each other. Illicit drug use, delinquency and criminal behaviour are closely associated for street living children. A national survey in the United States examined the relationship between substance abuse and delinquency. The study result showed that substance abuse had a strong correlation with criminal offence. But young age, poverty, weaken family bonding, inadequate love and affection etc was the more important correlate of criminal involvement (Harrison & Joseph). Another study in Lahore, Pakistan, observed the same finding of criminal offence followed by police arrest which was statistically significant by OR=3.3 and 95% CI=1.3-8.3 (Sherman & Plitt, 2005).

As street children were considered as unwanted burden to our society, civil society appears to be usually negative about these children. In this study, 61% of the participants (n=339) felt that community was indifferent towards them. Twenty four percent of them had a feeling of hatred against them by the society, 9% felt that they were somehow accepted by the community and 6% didn't have any idea about the attitude of the society. Similar study among street children in Lahore, Pakistan, found that drug use was significantly associated with the hatred attitude of community people with OR=5.1 and 95% CI=2-12.9 (Sherman & Plitt, 2005).

Substance Abuse:

Substance abuse is a common phenomenon in street children as observed by several communities throughout the world. Studies in developed or developing countries have emphasized that children are especially at risk of substance abuse, and this appears to be increasing. About 22% (n=122) children reported that they were exclusive smokers of 'bidi' or 'cigarette' and didn't have experience of any other substances in their lifetime. Prevalence of non-tobacco substance abuse was found to be 30% in this study (n=165). Considering exclusive bidi or cigarette smoking as well as non-tobacco substance abuse, the prevalence rate comes to 52% (n=287). A similar study in Delhi, reported that more than 50% street children were indulged in substances and smoking was the commonest form of abuse. The said study revealed that 8.5% abused chewable tobacco which were locally available under the brand name of 'Gutkha', 'Khaini', 'Musa ka Gul' etc (Tiwari, 2007). Basically these are sweet-flavored tobacco products made by betel nuts that attract street children easily as it gives some pleasure in their stressful life. Another study in Brazil documented a higher prevalence of non-injecting substance abuse (39%) and injecting drug abuse prevalence of 1.2% (Fernanda, Neiva, & Ramos, 2006). Some other studies have reported higher substance abuse rate of 69 - 81% among street children (Kipke, Montgomery & Simon 1997), (Abhay, Quazi, &Waghmare, 2008). Prevalence of substance abuse among street based children was reported from different continents. It was 74% in Europe, 51% in America, 46% in Middle East, 41% in Asia & Pacific region and 37% in Africa (Wright & Karnisky, 1993).

As smoking gets social acceptance during adulthood, children with exclusive bidi/cigarette smoking have not been focused & excluded in this present study. Only non-tobacco substance abusers, which do not have social acceptance even in adult life, have been considered in this study for further analysis. After arriving on the streets, children indulged into the habits of taking different types of substances to cope up with stressful street life. These children easily turned towards use of different substances as one of many survival strategies. After smoking, they started slowly the consumption of non-tobacco substances and in this study 30% of them (n=165) was found to indulge various non-tobacco substances on regular basis. In Nepal, it was found that one in ten (1 in10) teenagers were in the habit of non-tobacco substance abuse. Among them, 26% was reported to inhale and 5.4% with injecting habits (Rai & Ghimire, 2002). Another study in Pakistan considered substance abuse as a major coping mechanism among street children. In that study 67.1% reported to have recent drug use habits, whereas 17% didn't have the same. Substance abuse was associated with 13 year of age with OR of 3.0 and 95% CI = 1.3 – 7 (Sherman & Plitt, 2005). Similar study in Brazil has documented that, approximately 7 - 8 million unprotected & unsupervised children were living and working on the street and inhalants, marijuana, cocaine and Valium were commonly used substances among them (Incardia, 1998).

In view of unsupervised state of street children leading to hazardous way of living, the children usually initiate their substance abuse at an early age. In this study, the participants initiated substance abuse at the age of 6-10 year with the median age of 13 year. This could be due to cope up with their stressful street living. Similar study in Southern Brazil had also documented that the mean age of initiation of alcohol was 12 year, marijuana was under 13 year and cocaine was initiated among children less than 14 year age (Ferigolo, Barbosa, & Arbo, 2004). The present study showed that the rate of non-tobacco substance abuse was much higher in all age groups in males compared to females. It was also evident that the rate of non-tobacco substance abuse increases as age advances in males, whereas it is almost similar in 6 - 15 year and then it increases sharply with increase of age in females. Lower rate of abuse in female compared to male children can be related to difference in cultural acceptability (smoking is not culturally acceptable among Indian females), nature of work (jobs chosen by females require less energy unlike males), place of work (females tend to do indoor work) and peer pressure (males have a stronger influence between female and male children).

As reported by street children, the commonest non-tobacco substance abused by the children was 'Dendrite', a synthetic rubber, commercially available as an adhesive paste and used for fixing articles. Glue (Dendrite or Fevicol) is a popular intoxicant among street children throughout the nations of the developing world because it is very cheap, easily available even in small grocery shops and in present study, it was consumed by 43% study participants (n=104). Children prefer this because it diminishes pain, reduces fear, make them energetic and suppresses hunger whenever they need. Basically they inhale dendrite through mouth and the total process of inhalation was very interesting. At first, they purchase dendrite tube (available in different sizes and prices) as per their financial capacity. Then they squeeze the tube till it is exhausted and drop the full semi-liquid in a small piece of cloth and start to inhale through mouth. Within a few hours it evaporates and they become ready in the same way for the next tip. Other non-tobacco substances consumed by them was 'Ganja' [cannabis] (25%; n=61), Alcohol (16% (n=39), Brown Sugar (11%; n=27), Nitrazepum (2%; n=4) and pure Heroin (3%; n=7). A study among street children conducted in Nepal reported that 'Tidigesic' was the substance of choice among Nepali children (Rai, Ghimire, & Shrestha, 2002). Another study in Nigeria has found that the most commonly used substances were alcohol, colanut, tobacco and canabbis, because of its easy availability and cheaper cost (Morakinzi & Odejide, 2003). Similar study on substance abuse among street children in Southern Brazil found that the most frequent substances used by them was tobacco (58%) and alcohol (25%). Among them, 40% children abused inhalants on regular basis (Forster LM, 1996).

It was found from the study that dendrite was commonly abused by 58% (n=80) male and 18% (n=24) female participants. Substances like alcohol and ganja were consumed by both male (23%; n=31) and female (29%; n=8) participants. Other hard drugs like brown sugar, pure form of heroin and nitrazepum were consumed only by the male participants. Regarding frequency of consumption of non-tobacco substance per day, 61.2% (n=101) consumed it 1-2 times per day, 26.7% (n=44) consumed it 3-4 times and 8% (n=16) consumed for 5-6 times per day. Higher rate of consumption (7-8 times/day) was found among 1.8% children (n=3).

It was reported from the present study that most of the participants started consumption of non-tobacco substances by the pressure from their peer group which included adult members of their community also. Majority of the children (73%; n=121) were found to initiate substances by the pressure from their peer group followed by coping up with stressful situation. Similar finding was observed in a study from Mumbai, India, where 62.1% children used to take non-tobacco substance due to the pressure from their peer group (Abhay, Quazi, & Waghmare, 2008). Researchers have documented that peers have a high degree of influence only when the parents give up their traditional supervisory roles. So, proper parental supervision empowers children to overcome peer influence (Wright, Karnisky, & Wittig, 1993), (Blum, 1996). But in contrast, studies carried out in Columbia (Aptekar, 1988), Nepal

(Baker, Panter-Brick, & Todd, 1997), Indonesia (Gross, Landfried, & Herman, 1996) and Brazil (Rohde, Ferreira, Zomer, & Forster, 1998) highlighted the importance of the role of peer group on street living children. It was reported from these studies that bonding, caring and unconditional physical and emotional supports among peers have a positive effect on the mental health of street children that enabled them to better cope up with street life. As reported by the participants of the present study that adult people first time forced them to initiate substances. Once they turn out to be an addict, they themselves started off taking substances and cannot refrain from a single day without it. Only 13% of them (n=21) used to initiate substances out of curiosity, and 8% (n=13) was found to accept substances to overcome depression in this study. Six percent children (n=10) had to engage a long period for working and they started taking substances to over come heavy work load. A different scenario was observed in a study of Nepal that most of the abusers didn't use any hard type of substances like Heroin, but they preferred cheaper pharmaceutical substances like tidigesic (Rai & Ghimire, 2002). Unlike above studies, research among street children in Ireland documented that disrupted family life (not peer pressure) was found to be a major risk factor for substance abuse among these young children (Corrigan, 1986).

Sexual desire is said to be related with consumption of nature of chemical substances. For example, amphetamine is known to be sexually stimulant, whereas, heroin is sexually depressant. Alcohol in small dose increases the sexual desire. But it decreases sexual performance on higher doses. The present study observed neither increase nor decrease in sexual urge following drug abuse by the most of the study children ((57%; n=93). In contrast, children reported that after taking substances they were not in a mood to think about their sexual urge. They didn't even think about their daily livelihood also. After taking drugs, they just think for managing funds for their next dose. Only 25% (n=42) of them experienced an increased sexual urge after taking drugs, where as 18% of the participants (n=30) were so young that they didn't have any idea about sexual urge. Probably this is related with age, sexual system development and types/dose of drugs.

Because of unhygienic surroundings and poor living conditions along with substance abuse, health is a major concern to them. Withdrawal symptoms appear to be the commonest health problem related to substance abuse as reported by several studies. In this study, 33% abuser children (n=54) faced withdrawal problems like pain abdomen, insomnia, anorexia, vomiting, diarrhea, over sweating etc. this was caused by the discontinuation of non-tobbaco substances.

Counseling has psychological as well as physiological impact on abusers to get rid of bad habits of substance abuse. But in the present study, it was reported by only one participant (0.2%) who received counseling services. Majority (99%) of them (n=553) didn't have any access to counseling facilities. Hence, counseling service was found to be a felt need by many of the participants as well as adult community members who take care of them. Apart from substance abuse and its harmful effects, counseling needs to be based on awareness about personal health and nutrition, self and body protection, life skills, gender differentiation, physical changes, child sexual abuse, preventive health measures, awareness about family planning and knowledge about STDs & HIV/AIDS.

In the present study, certain factors found to be associated with non-tobacco substance abuse. Older children of 11 year or more, male children, orphan children, children having no contact with family members and children staying night at public places were found to be associated with non-tobacco substance abuse. This study has documented that substance abuse was much higher in older children of 11 year or more compared to younger ones and this difference was statistically significant by univariate analysis indicated by odds ratio (OR) of 2 and 95% confidence interval [CI] = 1 – 3.9. This indicates that older children were 2 times more at risk of indulging substance abuse compared to younger children. Similar finding was observed in a study in Lahor, Pakistan, where substance abuse was observed to be more prevalent among older children (13 year & above) compared to younger children indicated by OR =3.0 and 95% CI = 1.3 -7.0 and prevalence of arrest was more among substance abusers indicated by OR = 3.3 & 95% CI = 1.3 – 8.3 (Sherman & Plitt, 2005). Sex-wise, male children were 3.5 times more at risk of indulging substance abuse compared to females (OR =3.5 & 2.3; 95% CI = 2.2 – 5.8 & 1.4 – 4.1). This could be due to the factors like social rejection of substance abuse of females; stronger peer influence on male children as well as hard work that require more energy than usual and substance abuse might provide it. Orphan children had a higher substance abuse prevalence of 43.3% compared to children having one or both parents (23.6%). These orphan children were 2.4 times more at risk of indulging substance abuse (95% CI = 1.6 – 3.6) compared to children with parental guidance. This could be due to lack of parental supervision in orphan children as several studies have documented that peers have a high degree of influence only when the parents give up their traditional supervisory roles. Proper parental supervision empowers children to overcome peer influence (Wright & Karnisky, 1993); (Blum, 1996). Similar finding was documented in a study in Mumbai where children, who lived on the street alone were at a greater risk of substance abuse (P<0.05)

83

compared to children having parental supervision (Abhay, Quazi, &Waghmare, 2008). Another study in Brazil also observed the same findings (Forster & Tannhauser, 1996). Present study also reported that children spending night at public places (33.2%; n=156) were 4.2 times more at risk of substance abuse (95% CI= 1.9 – 9.2) than children living in private places (10.5%; n=9). This could be due to the fact that children staying at night in private places usually remain under supervision of some adult members, whereas children spending night at public places do not get similar supervision or guidance from responsible adults.

Researchers documented that certain factors help to reduce high risk behaviors among street children like strong bonding with parents, teachers and other adult members in the community, feeling valued, constructive school environment, family values, rules and expectations, religious beliefs and hope for the future. Lack of these protective factors, extreme poverty and fight for mere survival makes them susceptible to violence, drug abuse, trivial crime, and conflict with the law, sexual abuse, exploitation, neglect and commercial sex work (Reza & Kumar, 2005). Deprived of love, affection, sympathy and care - street children are victims of low self-esteem and emotional disorders; they find pleasure in some aspects of street life such as recreational sex, drug abuse etc. Thriving in an environment where risk is ever present facilitates development of a careless approach to danger and a craving for instant satisfaction resulting in recklessness and risk-taking behavior. It is clear that street children have some problems which are perhaps unique to them. Basically, they are extremely mobile in nature and their mobility depends on the availability of accommodation, work, safety, movement of their friends or gang members, police activity and also availability of substances.

In India, the problems of street children have never been focused by the governmental as well as non-governmental agencies at national or regional level. Specific strategies for intervention targeting street children are absent. These factors need to be addressed by the civil society members while planning for an appropriate intervention. Care must be taken by the appropriate authorities to reduce their stressful living situation as much as possible like providing night shelter facility, raising their awareness level etc. Although none of them was found to be an injecting drug user at the time of study but experience suggests that many of these street living drug abusers would become the street injecting abusers in future (**Sarkar, Mitra, & Bal, 2003**). An in-depth study is required to explore the possible ways to prevent this.

Sexual Abuse:

Like substance abuse, sexual abuse is too a common phenomenon among street children in all over the world. Most of these children cannot survive without offering sex as a new comer to the street life. World news in CNN reported that sexual abuse starts among these children at a very young age in some countries. Anything can happen to these children because people know that no one is there for their care and protection. Children can't avoid sexual abuse because they had to depend only on street for their living and new comers are welcomed as a street member by gang rape (CNN Interactive, 1996). Street children are easily abused sexually and in the present study, 9% of the studied children (n=51) were found to be abused sexually either by known or unknown persons. Higher prevalence of sexual abuse (16%) among street children was observed in a study in Colombo (Senanayake, Ranasinghe, & Balasuriya, 1994). But a study in USA documented much higher prevalence of sexual abuse (35%) among street based children (Tyler, Whitbeck, & Hoyt, 2004). Another study in Nigeria also reported that about 38% homeless female children were abused sexually within last three months from the time of study (Noell & Ochs, 2001). Other studies also found sexual exploitation among street living children (Gharaibe & Hoeman, 2003); (Silva, 2002).

In this study, male children had a higher sexual abuse prevalence (65%; n=33) compared to that of females (35%; n=18). Age-wise, highest prevalence of sexual abuse was observed in this present study in the age group of 11-15 year (39%; n=20). It was also found that as age increases sexual abuse prevalence decreases in male children but in females it shows a decreasing trend till 15 year and after that it sharply increases (figure - 47). This could be due to the fact that older female children are forced to surrender themselves to sexual exploitation, whereas males can resist and protect themselves to this when they grow older. A similar study in USA reported that almost half of the study participants were found to be abused sexually and females experienced significantly higher rates of sexual abuse compared to males (Kimberly & Tyler., 2002). Similarly, another study in Nigeria, found that 70% street based female children had been sexually abused, of them 17.2% had experienced penetrative sex (Ikechebelu & Udigwe, 2008). The present study highlighted that higher sexual abuse in male children of 15 year or less could be associated with the effect of substance abuse since young children were reported to be abused sexually mostly by the adult children with whom they share shelter and substances. Similar finding was documented in a study indicating

85

participants with a history of taking alcohol or marijuana had a significantly higher sexual abuse than those who did not have such behavior (Rew, Margaret, & M, 2001).

So far age of first sexual harassment is concerned, about half (49%; n= 25) of the studied children were abused in the early age of 6-10 year. The study has documented that younger children faced more sexual harassment compared to older one. This may be due to the fact that older children can protect themselves from sexual harassment and tackle the adverse situation. The older children could better assess people and became aware before occurrence of the incident. But younger children were innocent in nature and might not be able to judge the offender before the incidence come about and couldn't defend against such undesirable conditions.

Moreover, researchers explored that sexual assault is one of the most widespread forms of violence against girl children (Mont & Mc, 2007). According to World Health Organization (WHO), every one in four women experienced sexual violence globally by an intimate partner in their lifetime (World Health Organization, 2002). A national survey in USA documented that about 10% women have been victims of forced sex in their lifetime (Tizaden,P.;&Thoennes,N., 2002). Different studies have documented that sexual assault occurs along a range from unwanted touching to forceful sexual intercourse. The present study has observed that 69% children (n=35) faced hugging by opposite sex, 65% (n=33) faced forceful attempt to have sex against their will, 61% (n=31) faced forceful exposure of genitalia to the abuser. Other forms of abuse faced by them were forceful touching of genitalia (53%; n=27) and penetrative sex (23%; n=12) against their will. Female children, who intended for sex working in exchange of money, were four times more likely to have experienced penetrative sex in their lifetime than those who did not have such exposure (Zierler,Witbeek, &Mayer, 1996). Similar finding was reported from Herland that female sex workers were more likely to be raped (32.4%) than non-sex working (7.1%) females (El-Bassel, Schilling, & Irwin, 1997). Basically, forceful sexual abuse and rape are related to violence. This sexual violence increases HIV infection, directly through forced sex with an infected partner and indirectly through association with high risk behaviors, including multiple sex partners, inconsistent condom use, adequate intake of alcohol & substance abuse (Campbell, Baty, Ghandour, Stockman, Francisco,&Wagman, 2008); (Eby, Campbell, & Sullivan, 1995); (Kalichman, Williams, & Cherry, 1998); (Maman, Campbell, & Sweat, 2000); (Molitor & Ruiz, 2000); (Wingood & Diclemente, 2000); (Zierler,Witbeek, & Mayer,

1996). In addition of these factors, sexual violence is associated with some other factors also, that includes an increased risk of reproductive health problems like vaginal bleeding, fibroids, genital irritation, pain during intercourse, chronic pelvic pain, and urinary-tract infections (Eby, 1995), (Collett & Cordle, 1998) (Campbell, 2008). Furthermore, it may be related in emotional scarring, psychological stress and low self-esteem (Ellsberg, Jansen, Cooper, & Gilbert, 2008); (Kumar, Jeyaseelam, Suresh, & andAhuja, 2005); (Pico-Alfonso, Garcia-Linares, & Celda-Navarro, 2006); (Romero-Daza, Weeks, & andSinger, 2003).

From this study it was found that forceful penetrative sex was committed on 12 male children whereas no female children were reported this during the study period. This may be due to the fact that older males prefer to have penetrative sex with young male children than female children. Studied children reported that more than half of the participants (53%; n=27) were abused by single person at one time where as 27% of them (n=14) was reported to be abused by single person on multiple occasions and only 20% children (n=10) were abused in different occasions by different persons in their street lives. Some younger children reported that they were easily abused by some adult street members with whom they sleep at night for safe guardianship. Some of them were also abused by their group leader at the initial phase of street life. There was no chance of refusal. Because refused children would be isolated from the group, from sharing of food and shelter and would be targeted for further abuse. Street children were also targeted by unknown persons who abused them by giving false promise of food, shelter, job etc.

The present study identified certain factors like children of 10 year or less, orphan children, children having no contact with their parents and children spending night at public places were associated with sexual abuse. Younger children of 10 year or less had higher (21%) sexual abuse compared to older children (7.2%). Statistically, younger children were about 4 times more at risk of being sexually abused than older children (statistically significant both on univariate as well as multivariate analysis indicated by OR of 3.3 & 2.8 and 95% CI was 1.6 – 6.7 & 1.4 – 5.8 respectively). In the same way, orphan children had a higher sexual abuse of 27.6% (n=8) compared to their counterparts (8.2%; n=43) and univariate analysis revealed that orphan children were 4.2 times more at risk of being sexually abused than children with parents (OR = 4.2; 95% CI = 1.6 – 10). Probably this is related to lack of parental supervision and guidance in orphan children. Similarly, prevalence of sexual abuse among children having no contact with families was higher [16%; n=32] compared to children who had contacts with families (5%; n=19). Statistically, the former children were 3.4 times more at risk of being sexually abused than the later one (OR = 3.4 & 95% CI = 1.8 – 6.5). It was also observed that, children who usually spent night at public places faced more sexual abuse (10%; n=49) compared to their counterparts (2.4%; n=2) and this difference was also statistically significant indicated by OR = 4.8; CI = 1.2 – 41. So, factors like younger children (below 10 year), orphan children, children having no contact with families and children staying in public places at night might be considered as risk factors for sexual abuse in this study. Another research finding documented that sexual abuse was more among participants having history of taking alcohol and marijuana than those who did not have such history (chi 2 = 9.93, p < .01) (Rew & Horner, 2003).

The present study also reported that sexual abuse has certain effects on violence and substance abuse. Violence committed on sexually abused children was found to be more (53%) compared to the children without sexual abuse (34%). This difference was statistically significant indicated by OR=2.2 and 95% CI= 1.2 – 4. This shows that sexually abused children were 2.2 times more at risk of facing violence compared to their counterparts. In sexual abuse, sex is usually performed by force and against the will of the abused children. So, sexual abuse is usually related with either physical or mental or both form of violence and/or injury. When young boys are abused by the adult men, possibility of injury is higher due to forceful anal sex (because it is not the natural way of doing sex). More injury leads more bleeding episodes that has higher possibility of transmission of HIV infection if either partner is infected with HIV/STIs. This study has documented that 1% children (n=4) were related with such sexual activities with their male sex partners and majority of them performed it as an anal receptor (passive partner). It has also been documented that substance abuse was much higher (43%) among sexually abused compared to the same in non-abused ones (28%). This difference was also found statistically significant indicated by OR = 1.9 and 95% CI = 1 - 3.5.

Children, who are living on the street, need more information, education, knowledge and training to expand their awareness level about sexual abuse. They also need to develop skills in avoiding all types of abuses by empowering themselves. Government should take appropriate preventive measures to reduce all types of abuses against street living children.

Sexual Practice:

Disease transmission depends on inadequate knowledge, risk behavior, risk perceptions and risk practices. Regarding sexual practice, 65% children (n=360) reported to have no sexual relationship but 35% (n=194) had sexual relation with their partners. Of these children having relationship (n=194), 70% of them (n=136) had the experience of penetrative sex and among them, 13% (n=47) reported to visit sex workers within last one month where as 87% children (n=315) never visited sex workers till the time of this study. A study in Manila also documented that approximately 75,000 children live on the street and they were below poverty line. Due to their survival from severe poverty, approximately 20,000 children were forced to go for prostitution for their livelihood and among them a significant number of below 15 year children became infected with HIV (Tantoco, 1993). Similar study was conducted among street children attending sexually transmitted disease clinic in Guatemala where 94 children suffered from genital ulcer, 112 had genital herpes, 71 of them suffered from gonorrhea, 39 had human papillomavirus (HPV), 19 children suffered from vaginal trichomoniasis, 24 had chancroid, and 6 of them suffered from vaginal candidiasis (Solorzano & Arroyo, 1992).

As sexual abuse can be associated with higher rate of sexually transmitted infections (STIs), 13% study participants (n=73) reported to suffer from STIs within last six months. Of them, majority had a problem of discharge from their genital organ as indicated by clinical symptoms, examined by the study physician during this study. Substance abuse, sexual promiscuity, extreme poverty and low education place street children at high risk of acquiring Sexually Transmitted Infections (STIs) including HIV/AIDS. Several studies documented that sexual abuse facilitates transmission of STDs among street children (Gurumurthy, 2000); (Kricheff, 2007). The present study revealed that 1% of the studied population (n= 6) was infected with HIV and 4% (n=22) was infected with syphilis indicated by VDRL sero-positivity, considered as a composite marker of STIs in this study. Similar finding was also observed in Nigeria, where sexually transmitted infection followed by sexual abuse was 54.3% among street children (Ikechebelu & Udigwe, 2008). A similar study in Mumbai reported that, physical and sexual abuse among street children is very rampant that facilitates transmission of STDs among these children (Gurumurthy, 2000). In contrast, higher HIV transmission was observed in another study conducted in Philippines where prevalence of HIV among street children was 45% and the most common mode of transmission was through heterosexual intercourse. The high incidence of child sexual abuse and child prostitution in the Philippines results this high rate of HIV prevalence among adolescents and children below 15 year of age (Tantoco, 1993). Another study in Russia has also found a higher HIV prevalence of about 37% among street children (Tyler, Whitbeck, & Hoyt, 2004). Very little data on street children living with HIV/AIDS is available in South East Asia because data on this group is disaggregated and all data are 15-19 year old collected by national surveys. It was also known that street children are not core transmitters of HIV and therefore are not specifically tested to determine the levels of HIV in them. However, although knowing HIV prevalence levels of street children may be useful for advocacy but there is a danger that after knowing the actual scenario this may further stigmatize and marginalize these street children and subject them to greater abuse of their rights and freedoms. All above indicates that if the present situation continues, it can give rise to an epidemic of HIV in this population as earlier study conducted by NICED, documented that young female sex worker/girl children are more vulnerable for acquiring HIV infection during sexual exposure due to larger area of cervical ectopy, poor negotiating skill and low self esteem (Sarkar, Bal, & Mukherjee, 2006). This 1% HIV prevalence among street children of Kolkata city is a matter of concern and may be interpreted as the beginning of an epidemic in this population. Consequently, lack of immediate intervention in this group may lead to a bigger epidemic in near future. Considering all these factors, an urgent community-based intervention is the immediate need of the day with periodic monitoring and supervision.

Basic education and adequate knowledge about HIV/AIDS can prevent children from acquiring and transmitting diseases. About 53% of them (n=291) was found to have such knowledge but more than half of the participants (55%; n=159) didn't have any knowledge regarding HIV/AIDS. Of them, 40% children (n=115) were aware about unsafe sexual practice as one of the major route of HIV transmission. Few of them perceived that contaminated needle / syringe (3%, n=10) and unsafe blood transfusion (2.4%; n=7) are the route/s of HIV transmission. A similar finding was observed in a study in Turkey where more than half of the participants (56.8%) didn't have any knowledge regarding HIV/AIDS (Baybuga & Celik, 2004). Another pilot study was conducted among 100 street children in Ghana that has stated that 80% of them had poor knowledge of HIV/AIDS and 54% perceived themselves to be at risk for contracting HIV due to their street living situation (Anthony, Kumoji, & Rita, 2005). Other study of Turkey documented that street children had insufficient & incorrect knowledge about transmission and protection from HIV/AIDS. About 28.9% of them reported that individual hygiene was very important while 21.0% stated not sleeping with prostitutes, single marriages and condom use were very important ways to protect oneself from AIDS (Baybuga & Celik, 2004). Similar finding was also observed in a study in South Africa where all of the participants except two of them had heard about HIV/AIDS where as 93% had an idea that condom use can prevent HIV transmission and 68% were confident about healthy looking person could not carry HIV infection (Richter & Swart, 1995).

CONCLUSION

Street children require urgent intervention because of their risky life style, poor living conditions and marginalization. They are also considered as bridging population for the transmission of HIV/AIDS in the community. This study has documented their socio-demography, risk behaviour, risk perceptions on substance & sexual abuses as well as health related issues particularly blood borne infections and Sexually Transmitted Infections (STIs). It is alarming to note that the prevalence of sexual and substance abuses were 29.7% and 9.2% respectively. HIV prevalence was found to be 1% that requires immediate attention to prevent & control further spread of it within themselves as well as in the adjacent community.

The important factors that were found to be associated with substance abuse were older street children of 11 years or more, male participants, orphan children, children without contact with their families and children staying at public places. Similarly, factors like younger street children of 10 years or less, orphan children, children without contact with their families and children staying in public places at night were found to be more at risk of being sexually abused than their counter part.

At the international level, issues of street children have received much attention and several striking efforts have been made to eloquent them. Though India's performance is vital for the achievement of progress and development of street children since India forms more than a sixth of the world's population, out of which a good number of them are street children. But till date, India could not obtain that much effort that is required for a developing country for the betterment of street children. This is the time for commencement of appropriate strategies which will provide suitable environment for the welfare and development of these deprived children. Welfare service includes care and protection; development includes prevention & promotion for the better adjustment of children in the larger society. It will appear by the empowerment, participation and inclusion of street children in all the processes that children can use for self protection, survival, prevention and development. Since India is a resourceful country, it is felt need to mobilize all the resources properly to provide basic health care, education and shelter to these children in the direction of overall well being of them.

Considering all the above factors, it is necessary to develop a suitable community-based intervention programme targeted towards the street children to prevent and control all forms of sexual exploitation, sexual abuse, violence, prostitution, substance abuse and its consequences. Numerous programmes should be launched by various governmental bodies as well as by different voluntary organizations to provide services to street based children. Programmes should be broadly directed towards their health, nutrition, education, child labour, domestic as well as community violence, substance & sexual abuse and other support services.

Health is recognized as one of the basic rights of every child but unfortunately street children are unable to gain the access of it. For the prevention of vaccine preventable diseases, universal immunization programme should be considered under integrated child health programmes. To strengthen nutritional status, adequate mid-day meal should be provided.

Group living facilities should arrange to protect and avoid unsolicited sexual abuse. Existing laws on such abuse of street children must be enforced. There is also a need of suitable rehabilitation programme for drug abuse and sexually exploited children by educating & giving vocational training of the said community to protect them from social nuisances like unnecessary police harassment, tortured or beaten by the police due to their homelessness and staying at public places, criminally charged with vague offences, beggary & juvenile delinquency, branded as anti-social element etc. as well as to grow them like other main stream population.

Child welfare interventions usually focus on the overall well-being and development of the child within their family. Various researchers have found that children are best nurtured by the care, love and affection of parents that helps for their physical and mental development. In this purpose, economic support may be granted to their parents, so that parents can nurture their children properly instead of forcing them for economic support. Institutional care can be provided for orphan, abandoned and homeless children. In case of orphan and abandoned children, adoption method should be proverbial to give children decent environment. But it should be taken into account that legislation must be effective, persuasive and powerful in the process of adoption to escape child trafficking.

It is also found that children express their own views and ideas in the development of their community. So, before going to adopt any policies for children, a children's forum can be formed where they can raise voice against abuse, exploitation etc and can take appropriate policies beneficial for them.

As street children are vulnerable for acquiring and transmitting blood born infections (HIV/AIDS, STIs) due to their substance and sexual abuse behavour, suitable awareness programme for its prevention/control should be adopted by the department of health and other non-governmental health care providers. Moreover, some exclusive strategies should be developed to reduce their risk behavior and risk perceptions. Counselling services should be provided for their psychological well-being, so that children can easily cope up with their stressful street life.

At last, there are needs for coordination between different governmental organizations like department of Health, Education & Family Welfare as well as other public sectors who can meet the needs of the street children. As this is beyond the scope of a single authority like department of health & social welfare, hence it is necessary to join hands by all inter-related departments of Government as well as Non-Government organizations (Ministry of Health, Education & Social Welfare, Urban Development, Family Welfare, Railway Authority, Law & Order and different local NGOs etc). Without inter-sectoral collaboration, which is really the requirement for developing a comprehensive care package for street children based on the study findings, overall growth and development for these children would not be possible.

REFERENCE

1. Abhay, M., Quazi, S., & &Waghmare, L. (2008). Substance abuse among street childrenin Mumbai. *Vulnerable and Youth Studies , 3* (1), 42 - 51.

2. Abuse, T. N. (1994). *Fact Sheet on Child Sexual Abuse.* Huntsville, NRCCSA.

3. Aderinto, A. (2000). Social correlates and coping measures ofstreet-ch ildren: A comparative study ofstreet and non-street children in South-Western Nigeria . *Child Abuse and Neglect , 24* (9), 1199 - 1213.

4. Agnelli, S. (1986). *Street children: A growing urban tragedy.* London: Weidenfeld and Nicolson.

5. Aneci, R., Borba, E., & & Ebrahim, G. (1992). The street children of Recife: A study of their backgroun. *Journal of Tropical Pediatrics , 38* (1), 34 - 40.

6. Anthony, K., Kumoji, E., & Rita, D. (2005). HIV Knowledge and Sexual Risk Behaviors of Street Children in Takoradi,Ghana. *AIDS and Behaboir , 10* (2), 209 - 215.

7. Aptekar, L. (1988). *Street children in Kal, Durhami.* London, UK: Duke university Press.

8. AsiaOneNews(ANN). (2009). *Over half the street children in India sexually abused.* The Statesman.

9. Baker, R., Panter-Brick, C., & & Todd, A. (1997). Homeless street boys in Nepal: Their demography and lifestyle. *Journal of Comparative Family Studies , 28* (1), 129 - 146.

10. Ball, A. M. (1998, March 22). And Now My Soul Is Hardend:Abandoned Children in Soviet Russia, 1918-1930. *The Historian .*

11. Baybuga, M., & Celik, S. (2004). The level of knowledge and views of the street children/youth about AIDS in turkey. *International journal of Nursing Studies , 41* (6), 591 - 597.

12. Benalcazar, B. (1982). A study offif teen runaway patients. *Adolescence , 17* (67), 553 - 566.

13. Beyene, Y., & & Berhane, Y. (1997). Characteristics of street children in Nazareth, Ethiopia. *East African Medical Journal , 74* (2), 85 - 88.

14. Black, B., & & Farrington, A. (1997). Promoting life for Indinesia's street children. *AIDSLINK , 45*, 10 - 11.

15. Black, M. (1993). *Street and working children.* Summary Report. Innocenti Global Seminar, February 15 – 25, 1993, Florence, Italy: UNICEF.

16. Blum, R. (1996). Drug abuse prevention Through Family Intervention. *NIH Guide* , 13 - 96.

17. Boyer, D., & Fine, D. (1992). Sexual Abuse as a Factor in Adolescent Pregnancy and Child Maltreatment. *Family Planning Perspective , 24* (1), 4 - 11.

18. Campbell, J., Baty, M., Ghandour, R., Stockman, J., Francisco, L., & &Wagman, J. (2008).

19. (2001). *Challenges and opportunities - an UNICEF Report on Street Children.* New Delhi: UNICEF.

20. CNN. (1998, August 29). *http://www.cnn.com/WORLD/asiapcf/29/india.* Retrieved February 7, 2008, from www.cnn.com: http://www.cnn.com/WORLD/asiapcf/29/india.street. children/index.html

21. Collett, B., & Cordle, C. (1998). A comparative study of women with chronic pelvic pain,chronic non-pelvic pain and those with no history of pain attending general practitioners . *British Journal of Obstetrics and Gyneacology , 105* (1), 87 - 92.

22. Corrigan. (1986). Drug abuse in the Republic of Ireland: An overview. *Bulletin on Narcotics , 38* (1 - 2), 91 - 96.

23. De, L. (1998). The main cause ofil l health in urban children. *Health Education and Behavior , 25* (1), 46 - 59.

24. DelCol, L. (1848). *http://www.intute.ac.uk/cgi.* Retrieved August 25, 2008, from www.intute.ac.uk: http://www.victorianweb.org/history/workers1.html

25. DepartmentforInternationalDevelopment(DFID). (2003). *Mapping Population Groups Vulnerable to HIV/AIDS in West Bengal.* New Delhi: Taylor Nelson Sofres Mode Pvt. Ltd.

26. E.M.Salem, & F.AbdEl.latif. (2002). Sociodemographic Characteristics of Street Children in Alexandria. *Eastern Mediterranean health Journal , 8* (1).

27. Eby, K. (1995). Health effects of experiences of sexual violence for women with abusive partners. *Health care for Women International , 16*, 563 - 576.

97

28. Eby, K., Campbell, J., & Sullivan, C. (1995). Health effects of experiencesof sexual violence for women with abusive partners. *Health Care for Women International*, *16* (6), 563 - 576.

29. El-Bassel, N., Schilling, R., & Irwin, K. (1997). Sex trading and psychological distress among women recruited from the streets of Herland. *Psychology of Addictive Behavior* , *87* (1), 66 - 70.

30. Ellsberg, M., Jansen, H., Cooper, D., & Gilbert, L. (2008). Intimate partner violence and women's physical and mental health in the WHO multi-country study on women's health and domestic violence: an observational study. *The Lancet* , *371* (9619), 1165 - 1172.

31. Farrow, J., Deisher, R., & Brown, R. (1992). Health and health needs ofhomeless and runaway youth. *Journal of Adolescent Health* , *13* (8), 717 - 726.

32. Ferigolo, M., & Barbosa, F. A. (2004). Drug use prevalence at FEBEM, Porto Alegre. *Rev Bras Psiquiatr* , 6 - 10.

33. Fernanda, D., Neiva, S., & Ramos, M. (2006). Sexual and Drug Use Risk Behaviors among Children and Youth in Street Circumstances in Porto Alegre, Brazil . *AIDS and Behavior* , *10* (1), 57 - 66.

34. Finkelhor, D., Gerald, T., & Hotaling & Kersti, Y. (1988). *Stopping family violence.* Newbury Park,Calif, California, United States of America: Sage Publication.

35. Forster, L., & Tannhauser, M. (1996). Drug use among street children in Southern Brazil. *Drug Alcohol Dependence* , *43* (1 - 2), 57 - 62.

36. Ganeshan, A. &. (1996). *police Abuse & Killings of Street Children in India.* Delhi: Human Rights Watch.

37. Gharaibe, M., & & Hoeman, S. (2003). Health hazards and risks for abuse among child labour in Joran. *Journal of Pediatrics Nursing* , *18* (2), 140 - 147.

38. Gross, R., Landfried, B., & & Herman, S. (1996). Height & weight as a reflection ofthe nutritional situation of school aged children working and living in the streets of Jakarta. *Social Science & Medicine* , *43* (4), 453 - 458.

39. Gurumurthy, R. (2000). HIV/AIDS risk taking behavior among street children in Mumbai. *Internetional Conferance on AIDS* (pp. 9 - 14). Mumbai: International Conferance AIDS.

40. Hadi, A. (2000). Child abuse among working children in rural Bangladesh: Prevalence and determinants. *Public Health* , *114* (5), 380 - 384.

41. Harris, B. (2002). Child murders in Central America. *Lancet* , *360*, 1508.

42. Harrison, L., & Joseph, G. The intersection of drug use and criminal behaviour: Results from the National Household Survey on Drug Abuse. *Crime and Delinquency* , *38* (4), 422 - 443.

43. HumanRightsWatch. (1998). *Human Rights Watch World Report - 1998.* New York: Human Rights Watch.

44. Ikechebelu, J., & Udigwe, G. (2008). Sexual abuse among juvenile female street hawkers in Anambra state, Nigeria. *African Journal of Reproductive Health* , *12* (1), 111 - 119.

45. Incardia, J. S. (1998). Children in the streets of Brazil: drug use, crime, violenceand HIV risks. *Substance Use & Misuse* , *33* (7), 1462 - 1480.

46. JAMA. (1985). AMA diagnostic and treatement guidelines concerning child abuse and neglect. *The Journal of the American Medical Association* , 796-800.

47. Kalichman, S., Williams, E., & Cherry, C. (1998). Sexual coercion, domestic violence,and negotiating condom use among low income African, American women. *Journal of Women's Health* , *7* (3), 371 - 378.

48. Kimberly, A., & Tyler. (2002). Preparators of Early Physical and Sexual Abuse Among Homeless and Runaway adolescent. *Child Abuse and Neglect* , *26* (12), 1261 - 1274.

49. Kipke, M., Montgomery, S., & Simon, R. (1997). Life on streets. *Substance Use and Misuse* , 965-982.

50. Kricheff, D. (2007, November 12). *Reuter AlertNet-Study Finds 37.4% HIV Prevalence Among Street Youth in Russia.* Retrieved December 5, 2007, from Reuter AlertNet   Foundation.Website: http://www.alertnet.org/thenews/fromthefield/218478/119488173246.htm

51. Kumar, S., Jeyaseelam, L., Suresh, S., & andAhuja, R. (2005). Domestic violence and its mental health correlates in Indian women. *British Journal of Psychiatry* , *187*, 62 - 67.

52. Lalor, K. (1999). Street children a comparative perspective. *Child Abuse and Neglect* , *23* (8), 759 - 770.

53. Le, R. (1996). Street children in South Africa:findings from interviewes on the background of street children in Pretoria,South Africa. *MEDLINE* , *31* (122), 423 - 431.

54. Lipovsek, V. &. (2007). *Sampling Hard-to-Reach Population.* Washington,DC: Population Services International.

55. Maman, S., Campbell, J., & Sweat, M. (2000). The intersections of HIV and violence:directions for futureresearch and interventions. *Social Science and Medicine*, *50* (4), 459 - 478.

56. Merrill, J., & Peters, L. (2001). *Adolescent psychiatry in clinical practice*. London: Arniold Publisher.

57. Mervyn, F. (2002). *Constituting Human Rights: Global civil society and the society of democratic states*. London: Routledge.

58. Moazzam, A., Saqib, S., & Hiroshi, U. (2004). Street children in Pakistan: A situational analysis of social conditions and nutritional status. *Social Science & Medicine*, *59*, 1707 - 1717.

59. Molitor, F., & Ruiz, J. (2000). History of forced sex in association with drug use and sexual HIV risk behaviors, infections with STDs and diagnostic medical care. Results from the young women survey. *Journal of interpersonal violence*, *15*, 262 - 278.

60. Mont, D., & Mc, G. (2007). Commercial "Partnering": sex Work, Trafficking and Pornography. In D. Mont, & G. Mc, *Sexual partnering, Sexual Practices and Health* (pp. 99 - 151). Springer US.

61. Morakinzi, J., & Odejide, A. O. (2003). A community based study of patterns of psychoactive substance abuse among street children in a local government area of Nigeria. *Drug Alcohol Depend*, 113-124.

62. NewWorldEncyclopedia. (2006, April 26). *http://www.newencyclopedia.org*. Retrieved September 22, 2008, from www.newworldencyclopedia.org: http://www.newencyclopedia.org/entry/kolkata

63. Noell, J., & & Ochs, L. (2001). Relationship ofsexual orientation to substance abuse, suicidal ideation, suicide attempts and other factors in a population of homeless adolescents. *Journal of Adolescent Health*, *29* (1), 31 - 36.

64. Pandhi, R., Khama, K., & & Sekhri, R. (1995). STD in Children. *Indian Pediatrics*, *32*, 27-30.

65. Parker, L. (2002). Street children and child labour around the world. *The Lancet*, *360* (9350), 2067 - 2071.

66. PATH. (2009, May). *Technology Solutions for Global Health: Rapid Tests for Cervical Cancer*. Retrieved June 8, 2009, from www.path.org: http://www.path.org/files/TS_update_cervical_cancer.pdf

67. Pico-Alfonso, M., Garcia-Linares, M., & Celda-Navarro, N. (2006). The impact of physical, psychological and sexual intimate male partner violence on women's mental health: depressive symptoms, posttraumatic stress disorder, state anxiety,and suicide. *Journal of Womwn's Health*, *15* (5), 599 - 611.

68. Pinto, J., & Ruff, A. P. (1994). HIV Risk Behaviour and Medical Status of Underpriviledge Youths in Belo horizonte. *Journal of Adolescent Health , 15* (2), 179 - 185.

69. Polat, O. (2009, April). *http://www.adlitip.org/.* Retrieved May 25, 2009

70. Rai, A., & Ghimire, P. &. (2002). *Glue Sniffing Among Street Children in the Kathmandu Valley.* Kathmandu: Child Works in Nepal.

71. Report, U. (2001). *Challenges and opportunities - an UNICEF Report on Street Children.* New Delhi: UNICEF.

72. Rew, L., & & Horner, D. (2003). Personal strengths of homelessness adolescents living in a high-risk environment. *Advances in Nursing Sciences , 26* (2), 90 - 101.

73. Rew, L., Margaret, T., & M, L. (2001). Sexual abuse, Alcohol and other drug use and suicidal behavior in homeless adolescents. *Comprehensing Pediatric Nursing , 24* (4), 225 - 240.

74. Reza, M., & Kumar, T. &. (2005). *Struggle for survival:A study on Needs and Problems of the Street and Working Children in Sylhet City.* Sylhet: Shahjad University of Science & Technology.

75. Riberio, M. (2008). Street children and their relationship with the police. *International Nursing Review , 55* (1), 89 - 96.

76. Richter, L., & Swart, K. (1995). AIDS risk among street children and youth: implications for intervention. *South African Journal of Psychology , 25* (1), 8 - 31.

77. Richter,L.M. (1991). *Street children in South Africa: General Theoritical introduction: Society, family and childhood.* Paper presented at the first national workshop of street-wise,Jojannesburg

78. Rohde, L., Ferreira, M., Zomer, A., & Forster, L. (1998). The impact of living on the streets on latency children's friendships. *Revista de Saude Publica , 32* (3), 273 - 280.

79. Romero-Daza, N., Weeks, M., & andSinger, M. (2003). Violence,drugs and street-level prostitution in inner-city Hartford, Connecticut. *Medical Anthropology , 22* (3), 233 - 259.

80. Sarkar, K., Bal, B., & Mukherjee, R. e. (2005). Epidemiology of HIV infection among brothel-based sex workers in Kolkata,India. *Journal Health Population Nutrition , 23* (3), 231 - 235.

81. Sarkar, K., Bal, B., & Mukherjee, R. (2006). Epidemic of HIV coupled with hepaitis C virus among injecting drug users of Himalayan West Bengal, Eastern india, Bordering Nepal, Bhutan and Bangladesh. *Substance Use Misuse , 41* (3), 341 - 352.

82. Sarkar, K., Bal, B., & Mukherjee, R. (2006). Young age is a risk factor for HIV among female sex workers- An experience from India. *Journal of Infection*, *53* (4), 255 - 259.

83. Sarkar, K., Das, N., & Panda, S. (1993). Rapid spread of HIV among Injecting drug users in north-eastern states of India. *Bulletin on Narkotics*, 91 - 105.

84. Sarkar, K., Mitra, S., & Bal, B. e. (2003). Rapid spread of hepatitis C and needle exchange programme in Kolkata,India. *Lancet*, *361* (9365), 1301 - 1302.

85. Senanayake, M., Ranasinghe, A., & & Balasuriya, C. (1994). Street Children: A preliminary study. *Archives of Pediatrics and Adolescent Medicine*, *148* (7), 704 - 708.

86. Sharma, O., & Carl, H. (2007). *Population of Delhi UA, Greater Mumbai UA, and Kolkata UA, 1991 and 2001 Censuses and 2007 Estimate.* New Delhi: PopulationReferenceBureau.

87. Sherman, S., & Plitt, S. &. (2005). Drug use, street survival and risk behaviour among street children in Lahor, Pakistan. *Journal of Urban Health*, *82* (3 suppl 4), 113 - 124.

88. Silva, T. (2002). Preventing child exploitation on the streets on the Philippines. *The Lancet*, *360* (9344), 1507.

89. Solorzano, E., & Arroyo, G. (1992). Sexually transmitted diseases in Guatamala city street children. *Rev Col Med Cir Guatem*, *2*, 48 - 51.

90. Subedi, G. (2002). *Trafficking & sexual abuse among street children in Kathmandu.* Kathmandu: International Labour Organization & International Programme on the Elimination of Child Labour.

91. Tantoco, F. (1993). Philipines: street children, children at risk. *Children Worldwide*, *20* (2 - 3), 35 - 7.

92. Terredes, H. (2002). *Needs assessment of children working in streets of Kabul.* Kabul: Central Statistics office of Afghanistan.

93. Tizaden,P.,&Thoennes,N. (2000).*Full Report of the Prevalence, Incidence, and Consequences of Violence Against Women: Findings From The National Violence Against Women Survey.*Washington, DC:National Institute of Justice, Centers for Disease Control and Prevention.

94. Tiwari, P. (2007). Life on Streets. *Indian Journal of Pediatrics* .

95. Tyler KA, Whitbeck, L.B., Hoyt, D.R. & Cauce, A.M. (2004). Risk factors for sexual victimization among male and female homeless and runaway youth. *Journal Interpers Violence*, 19(5) 503-520.

96. UNICEF. (2009, January). *http://www.children fo.org/labour.html*. Retrieved May 25, 2009, from http://www.children fo.org/labour.html

97. UNICEF. (2001). *Profiting from abuse.* New York: The United Nations Children's Fund.

98. UNICEF. (March,2002). *Rapid Assessment of Street Children In Lusaka.* University of Zambia. Zambia: Project Concern International Zambia.

99. Watch, H. R. (1996, November). Police Abuse and Killings of Street Children in India. Washington, New York, United States of America.

100.   West, A. (2003). *http://www.adb.org/Street Children Asia Pacific/SCfinal.* Retrieved September 21, 2008, from www.adb.org: http://www.adb.org/Street Children Asia pacific/SC final.PDF

101.   West, A. (2003). *Poverty and Social Development papers.* Retrieved September 21, 2008, from At the Margins: Street children in Asia and the Pacific: http://www.adb.org/Street Chidren Asia Pacific/SC final.PDF

102.   West, A. (2003). *Street Children in Asia and the Pacific.* Regional and Sustainable Development Department. Asian Development Bank.

103.   White, C. (2002). Being, becoming and relationship:Conceptual challenges o fa child rights approach in development. *Journal of International Development , 14,* 1095 - 1104.

104.   WHO. (1997). *Child Abuse and Neglect.* World Health Organization.

105.   WHO. (2002). *World report on violence and health.* Geneva: World Health Organization.

106.   Wingood, G., & Diclemente, R. (2000). Identifying the prevalence and correlates of STDs among women residing in rural domestic violence shelters. *Women and Health , 30* (4), 15 - 26.

107.   WorldStreetChildrenNews. (2001). *Kyrgyzstan:IRIN Focus on Street Children in Bishkek.* Bishkek: Asia and pacific StreetKid News.

108.   Wright, D., & Karnisky, D. W. (1993). Health and social conditions of street children in Honduras. *American Journal of Diseases of Children , 147,* 282.

109.   Zierler, S., Witbeek, B., & & Mayer, K. (1996). Sexual violence against women living with or at risk for HIV infection. *American Journal of Preventive Medicine , 12* (5), 304 – 310.

BIBLIOGRAPHY

1.	Kudrati M.	2008	A study of the daily lives of the street children in Khartoum , Sudan , with intervention-recommendations, page:439-48.
2.	Ahmadhaniha HR	2007	The frequency of sexual abuse and depression in a sample of street children of one of deprived districts of Tehran, page: 23-35.
3.	Sherman SS	2005	Drug use, street survival, and risk behaviors among street children in Lahore , Pakistan, page:113-124 .
4.	Seth R	2005	Street and working children of Delhi , India , misusing toluene: an ethnographic exploration, page: 1659-79.
5.	Pagare D	2005	Sexual abuse of street children brought to an observation home, page: 134-39.
6.	Jutkowitz JM	1997	Drug use in Nepal : the view from the street, page: 987-1004.
7.	Nigam S	1994	Street children of India -- a glimpse, page: 63-67.
8.	Connolly M	1993	Manila street children face many sexual risks, page: 24-5.
9.	Kahabuka FK	2006	Oral health knowledge and practices

among Dar es Salaam institutionalized former street children aged 7-16 years, page: 174-178.

10.	Worthman CM	2008	Homeless street children in Nepal : use of allostatic load to assess the burden of childhood adversity, page:233-255
11.	Olgar S	2008	Electrocardiographic and echocardiographic findings in street children known to be substance abusers, page: 56-61.
12.	Kissin DM	2007	HIV seroprevalence in street youth, St.Petersburg, Russia, page: 2333-40.
13.	Admadkhaniha HR	2007	The frequency of sexual abuse and depression in a sample of street children of one of deprived districts of Tehran, page: 23-35 .
14.	Greksa LP	2007	Growth and health status of street children in Dhaka , Bangladesh, page: 51-60 .
15.	Pinzon-Rondon AM	2006	Street child work in Latin American capitals, page: 363-72.
16.	Vahdani P	2006	Prevalence of hepatitis B, hepatitis C, human immunodeficiency virus, and syphilis among street children residing in southern Tehran , Iran, page: 153-155 .
17.	Dooan MC	2006	The oral health status of street children in Adana , Turkey, page: 92-96 .
18.	Wutoh AK	2006	HIV knowledge and sexual risk behaviors of street children in Takoradi, Ghana, page: 209-15 .
19.	Ali M	2005	Illness incidence and health seeking

			behaviour among street children in Rawalpindi and Islamabad , Pakistan - a qualitative study, page: 525-32.
20.	Pagare D	2004	Risk factors of substance use among street children from Delhi, page: 221-5.
21.	Ruiz J	1994	Street youth in Colombia: lifestyle, attitudes and knowledge, page: 12-4.
22.	Le Roux J	1996	Street children in South Africa: findings from interviews on the background of street children in Pretoria, South Africa, page: 423-31.
23.	Forster LM	1996	Drug use among street children in southern Brazil, page: 57-62.
24.	Bernier M	1995	Street children and AIDS in Haiti, page: 125-30
25.	Filqueires A	1992	Taking health promotion on to the streets, page: 7
26.	Baybuqa MS	2004	The level of knowledge and views of the street children/youth about AIDS in Turkey, page: 591-597.
27.	Tantoco FG	1993	Philippines: street children, children at risk, page: 35-37.
28.	Richter L M	1995	AIDS-risk among street children and youth: implications for intervention, page: 31-38.
29.	Solórzano E	1992	Sexually transmitted diseases in Guatemala City street children,

page: 48-51.

30.	Ribeiro M O	2008	Street children and their relationship with the police, page: 89-96.
31.	Inciardi J A	1998	Children in the streets of Brazil: drug use, crime, violence, and HIV risks, page: 1461-80.
32.	Agnelli	1986	Street children: a growing urban tragedy: a report for the Independent Commission on International Humanitarian Issues, London, page: 123.
33.	Aptekar, Lewis.	1994	Street children in the developing world: a review of their condition, Cross-Cultural Research, Page: 195-224.
34.	Balanon, Lourdes G.	1989	Street children: strategies for action, Child Welfare, page: 159-166.
35.	Barker,Gary	1991	Exploited entrepreneurs: street and working children in developing countries, New York,USA, page: 17.
36.	Barrette,Michel J.	1995	Street children need our care, Pretoria, South Africa, page: 172.
37.	Bemak Fred	1996	Street researchers: a new paradigm redefining future research with street children, childhood, page: 147-156
38.	Black, Maggie	1993	Street and working children: summary report of the Innocenti

Global Seminar on working and
street children, Florence, Italy,
page: 56.

| 39. | Burt, Martha R. | 1991 | Alternative methods to estimate the number of homeless children and youth: final report, Washington, D.C, page: 46. |

| 40. | Cosgrove J | 1990 | Towards a working definition of street children, International social work, page: 185-192. |

| 41. | Ensign J | 2003 | Ethical issues in qualitative health research with homeless youths, Journal of Advanced Nursing, page: 43-50. |

| 42. | Royal Tropical Institute, Amsterdam, | 1996 | European Conference on Street Children Worldwide, page: 129. |

| 43. | Greenblatt, Milton | 1993 | Life-styles, adaptive strategies, and sexual behaviors of homeless adolescents, Hospital and Community Psychiatry, page: 1177-1180. |

| 44. | Harmse Marthi | 2002 | Action research on operations research for street children, Systemic Practice and Action Research, page: 37-49. |

| 45. | Horowitz Sandra V | 1994 | Constructive conflict management and |

coping in homeless children and adolescents, page: 85-98.

46.   Hutz, Claudio S   1995   Ethical issues in research with street children, page:16.

47.   Kaminsky, Donald C   1995   Street children, World Health, page:26 - 27

48.   Lalor Kevin J.   1999   Street children: a comparative perspective, page: 759-770.

49.   Leroux, Johann   1996   The worldwide phenomenon of street children: conceptual analysis, page:965-971.

50.   Lucchini, Riccardo   1993   Street children: a complex reality, page:23.

51.   Lucchini, Riccardo   1994   The street girl: prostitution family and drug, page: 41.

52.   Maclaughlin, Wendy W.   1991   Homeless children's perspective as a whole, page: 73.

53.   Molnar, Janice M   1990   Constantly compromised: the impact of homelessness on children, page: 109-124.

54. Panter-Brick, Catherine   2001   Street children and their peers:

			Perspective on homelessness, poverty, and health, page: 83-97.
55.	ROMERO, F.	1991	Children of the streets, page:16-18.
56.	World Association of Girl Guides and Girl Scouts	1992	Street children: struggling against the odds, world issues, page: 8.
57.	TAYLOR, Max	1996	Rethinking the problem of street children: parallel causes and interventions, page:236
58.	VAN BEERS, Henk	1996	A plea for a child-centered approach in research with street children, childhood, page: 195-201.
59.	International Catholic Bureau	1991	The sexual exploitation of children, page:199
60.	English, Abigail	1991	Runaway and street youth at risk for HIV infection, page: 504-510.
61.	HOLDEN, E. Wayne	1995	The mental health of homeless children, page: 165-178.
62.	LOWRY, Christopher	1995	Reaching street youth on substance abuse, page: 131-134.
63.	VELASQUEZ, E.	1991	The street children and the services for the drug abuse treatment access and

accessibility, page: 44.

64.   Healey, Justin   2005   Child sexual abuse, page: 44

65.   Bayes, Helen   2004   Children's' rights have long roots,
                                          page:16-18

66.   Higgins, Daryl J   2001   A case study of child sexual abuse
                                          within a church community, page: 5-19.

67.   Bergen   2004   Sexual abuse, anti-social behaviour &
                                          substance use: gender differences in
                                          young community adolescents, page: 34-
                                          41.

68.   Dodd   2006   Current policies & practices addressing
                                          the impact of drug and alcohol misuse
                                          on   children and families, page: 49.

69.   Harbin   2006   Secret lives, growing with substance:
                                          working with children and young
                                          people affected by familial substance
                                          misuse, page:146.

70.   Bourdillon   1994   Street children in Harare, Africa,
                                          page: 4.

71.   Mikulak, M.   2003   Street Children in Kenya: Voices of
                                          Children in Search of a Childhood,
                                          page: 390-392.

72.   O'Kane, Claire   2003   Street and Working Children's
                                            Participation in Programming for their
                                            Rights, page: 31.

73.   Panter-Beick   2002   Street Children, human rights and
                                            public health: A Critique and future
                                            Directions, page: 147-171.

74.   Richter, Linda M   2003   The Psychological Assessment of
                                            South African Street Children, page: 13.

75.   Swart, Jill   1990   Malunde The Street Children of
                                            Hillbrow, page: 203-205.

76.   Thomas de Benitez   2003   Reactive, Protective, and Rights-Based
                                            Approaches in Work with Homeless
                                            Street Youth, page: 13.

77.   Volpi, Elena   2003   Street Children: Promising Practices
                                            and Approaches, page: 13.

78.   Abdelgalis, S   2004   Household and family characteristics of
                                            Street Children in Aracajua, Brazil,
                                            page: 817-20.

79.   Aptekar, L   2003   Methodological Implications of
                                            Contextual Diversity in Research on
                                            Street Children, page: 13.

80.   Bar-On, A   1997   Criminalizing Survival: Images &
                                            Reality of Street Children, page: 63-78.

| 81. | Beazley, H | 2003 | The Construction & Protection of Individual & Collective Identities by Street Children & Youth in Indonesia, page: 13. |

82. Conticini, A 2006 Escaping Violence, Seeking Freedom: Why Children in Bangladesh Migrate to the Street, page: 241-54.

83. Human Rights Watch 2006 Street Children in the Democratic Republic of Congo, page: 18.

84. Hussein, N 2005 Street Children in Egypt. Group Dynamics & Subculture Constituents.

85. Mikulak, M 2003 The Social Construction of Disposable Children: Street and Working Children in Curvelo, Brazil, page: 63.

86. Raffaelli, M 1999 Homeless and Working Street Youth in Latin America, page: 7-28.

87. Rizzini, I 1996 Street Children: An Excluded Generation in Latin America, page: 215-233.

88. Stephenson, S 2001 Street Children in Moscow, page: 530-547.

89.	Young, L	2004	Journeys to The Street, The Complex Migration Geographies of Uganda Street Children, page: 471- 488.
90.	Alexander, S	1984	Improving sex education programs for young adolescents: parents views, page: 251-257.
91.	Yamamoto, J	1997	Transcultural Child Development: psychological assessment and treatment, page: 617-630.
92.	UNICEF, Annual report of the United Nations Children's Fund	1992	Health for All in the 21st Century,Genev
93.	Fisher, D	1986	Parent child communication about sex and young adolescents sexual knowledge and attitudes, page: 517-527.
94.	Geasler, M	1995	Sexuality education of young children, Parental concerns, page: 164-188.
95.	Munevver, Turkmen	2004	A descriptive study of Street Children living in a Southern city of Turkey, page: 131-136.
96.	Kipke, MD	1997	Homeless youths and their exposure to & involvement in violence while living

on streets, page: 360-367.

97.   Turkmen, M   1998   The socio-demographic conditions of
                                      children working on the streets in
                                      Adana, page: 509-515.

98.   Tuzun, B   1999   Substance abuse in children: an
                                      investigation, page: 17-21.

99.   Polat, O   1999   Street children in Turkey, page: 1-9.

100. Senayake, MP   1998   Street children preliminary study,
                                      page: 191-193.

101. Gross, R   1996   Height & weight as a reflection of
                                      Nutritional situation of school aged
                                      children working and living in the
                                      streets of Jakarta, page: 453-458.

102. Ayaya, SO   2001   Health Problems of Street children in
                                      Eldoret, Kenya, page: 609-624.

103. Morakinyo, J   2003   A community based study of patterns
                                      of psychoactive substance use among
                                      street children in a local Government
                                      area of Nigeria, page: 109-116.

104. Kushwaha, KP   1992   Prevalence & abuse of psychoactive

substances in children and adolescents, page: 208-261.

105.	Kang, M	2002	Substance abuse in Teenagers, Trends and consequences, page: 8-11.
106.	Rew, L	2001	Sexual abuse, alcohol and other drug use and suicidal behaviours in homeless adolescents, page: 225-240.
107.	Tripathi, BM	1999	Substance abuse in children and adolescents, page: 569-575.
108.	Susan, S	2005	Drug use, street survival, and risk behaviours among street children in Lahore, Pakistan, page: 113-124.
109.	Marina Del Rey	2000	Street Children & Drug Abuse: Social & Health consequences, page: 17-19.
110.	Apt, N.A.V	1991	Street children in Accra: a survey report. Department of Sociology, University of Ghana.
111.	Barker, G	1993	Knowledge, attitude and practices among street youth, page: 41-42.
112.	Boyden, J	1991	Children of the Cities, London: Zed Books Ltd

113. Janus, M.D   1987   Adolescent Runaways, Toronto:
                                        Lexington Books

114. Kaime-Atterhog, W   1996   Street children and prostitution: The
                                        situation in Kenya, page: 27-32.

115. Kufeldt, K   1987   Kids on the street, they have something
                                        to say: survey of runaway and homeless
                                        youth, page: 53-61.

116. Korbin, J.E   1983   Child Abuse and Neglect, Cross
                                        Cultural Perspectives, University of
                                        California Press.

117. Raffaelli, M.R   1993   Sexual practices and attitudes of street
                                        youth in Belo Horizonte, Brazil,
                                        page: 661-670.

118. Raffaelli, M.E   1995   HIV- related knowledge and risk
                                        behaviours of street youth in Belo
                                        Horizonte, Brazil, page: 287-297.
119. Winn, M   1984   Children without Childhood,
                                        Harmondaworth: Penguin.

120. Mati, J.K   1989   A review of adolescent health,
                                        page: 19-22.

121. UNICEF Report   2007   Street children definition

122. Merrill, J   2001   Adolescent psychiatry in clinical
                                       practice, page:150-176.

123. Pandhi, R.K   1995   STD in children, page: 27-30.

124. Jama   1985   AMA diasnostic and treatment
                                       guidelines concerning child abuse and
                                       neglect, page: 796-800.

125. Pinto, J.A   1994   HIV risk behaviour and medical status
                                       of Underprivileged youths in Belo
                                       Horizonte, Brazil, page: 179-185.

126. Ray, S.K   1999   Nutritional status of pavement dwellers
                                       children in Calcutta city, page: 49-54.

127. Remington, F   1993   The forgotten ones. A story of street
                                       children and schooling in South Asia,
                                       page: 40-42.

128. Coward Bucher, C. F 2008   Toward a needs-based typology of
                                       homeless youth, page: 549-554.

129. Solorio, M.R   2008   Predictors of sexual risk behaviours
                                       among newly homeless youth: a
                                       longitudinal study, page: 401-409.

130. Hosny, G   2007   Environmental behavioural
                                       modification programme for street

children in Alexandria, Egypt,
page: 1438-48.

131. Riberio, M.O   2008   Street children and their relationship
with the police, page: 89-96.

132. Whitbeck, L.B   2007   Victimization and posttraumatic stress
disorder among runaway and homeless
adolescents, page: 721-34.

133. Worthman, C.M   2008   Homeless street children in Nepal: use
of allostatic load to assess the burden of
childhood adversity, page: 233-55.

134. Rew, L   2008   Caring for and connecting with
homeless adolescents, page: S42-51.

135. Lankenau, S.E   2005   street careers: homelessness, drug use
and sex work among young men who
have sex with mwn, page: 10-18.

136. Kelly, K   2007   Health and street/ homeless youth,
page: 726-36.

137. Rew, L   2007   Outcomes of a brief sexual health
intervention for homeless youth,
page: 818-32.

138. Grant, R   2007   The health of homeless children
revisited, page: 173-87.

139. Slesnick, N   2008   The impact of an integrated treatment on HIV risk behaviour among homeless youth: a randomized controlled trial, page: 45-59.

140. Stewart, M   2007   Support intervention for homeless youths, page: 203-207.

141. Richards, R   2007   Environmental, parental and personal influences on food choice, access and overweight status among homeless children, page: 1572-83.

142. Tyler, K.A   2006   Trading sex: voluntary or coerced? The experiences of homeless youth, page: 208-16.

143. Rice, E   2007   Pro-social and problematic social network influences on HIV/AIDS risk behaviours among newly homeless youth in Los Angeles, page: 697-704.

144. Rosenthal, D   2007   Changes over time among homeless young people in drug dependency, mental illness and their co-morbidity, page: 70-80.

145. Roy, E   2007   Trends in injection drug use behaviors over 10 years among street youth,

page: 170-175.

146. Tyler, K.A   2007   Sexual health of homeless youth:
                                          prevalence and correlates of sexually
                                          transmissible infections, page: 57-61.

147. Kahabuka, F.K   2006   Oral health Knowledge and practices
                                          among Dar es Salaam institutionalized
                                          former street children aged 7-16 years,
                                          page: 174-178.

148. Johnson R.J   2006   The relationship between childhood
                                          sexual abuse and sexual health
                                          practices of homeless adolescents,
                                          page: 221-234.

149. De Carvalho, F.T   2006   Sexual and drug use risk behaviors
                                          among children and youth in street
                                          circumstances in Porto Alegre, Brazil,
                                          page: S57-66.

150. Vahdani, P   2006   Prevalence of hepatitis B, Hepatitis C,
                                          human immunodeficiency virus and
                                          syphilis among street children residing
                                          in southern Tehran, Iran,page:153- 155.

151. Milburn, N.G   2006   Cross-national variations in behavioral
                                          profiles among homeless youth,

page: 63-76.

152. Rosenthal, D   2006   Why do homeless young people leave
                                          home? Page: 281-285.

153. Steensma, C   2005   Cessation of injection drug use among
                                          street- based youth, page: 622-637.

154. Nyamathi, A.M   2005   Hepatitis C virus infection, substance
                                          use and mental illness among homeless
                                          youth: a review, page: S34-40.

155. Whitbeck, L.B   2006   Food insecurity among homeless and
                                          runaway adolescents, page: 47-52.

Picture-1: Temporary sleeping place of street children

Picture-2: Street children eating leftover food of train passengers

Picture-3: Study children collecting empty bottle from Railway station

Picture-4: A street child taking rest before loading goods in a train

Picture-5: Rag picking by the study participants

Picture-6: Children getting ready for smoking 'Ganja'

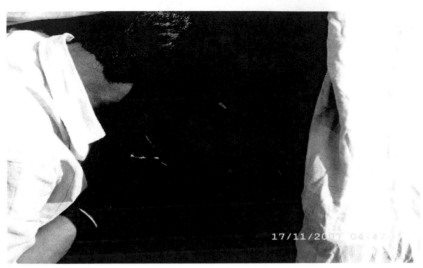

Picture-7: Children inhaling brown sugar on the street

Study on Street children

A: - Demography:

1. ID No: _____   Date: _____
2. Age: _____   3. Sex: M / F
4. Education: 1) Formal 2) Informal 3) None; [specify]_____
5.1. Currently attending school?   Yes / No; 2) If no,why_____
6. Marital status: 1) Unmarried,   2) Married,   3) Married but separated,   4) Divorcee,
           5) Widow / widower
7. 1. Are you engaged in any type of work at present?   Yes / No;
7. 2. If 'Yes' then specify_____
8. If you are jobless, then who support/s you & how? _____
9. 1. No of working days/ month: _____;   2. No of jobless days/ month: _____;
10. Total income from this work /day _____ /week _____ /month _____
11. Why are you engaged in this work? 1) To support self,   2) To help family members,
     3) Both,   4) Others (specify) _____
12. **1.** Status of your father: 1) Alive, 2) Dead, 3) Not known;   **2.**Working/Not working;
     3. Nature of job_____
13. **1.** Status of your mother: 1) Alive, 2) Dead, 3) Not known;   **2.**Working/Not working;
     3. Nature of job_____
14. **1.** Status of your spouse: 1) Alive, 2) Dead, 3) Not known;   **2.** Working/N W;
     3. Do you get financial support? Yes / No
15. Present place of sleep at night? 1) Public place   2) Private place owned by self
                              3) Private place owned by others
16. 1. Do you sleep under shelter?   Yes / No; 2. If 'Yes' then - 1) Temporary 2) Permanent
17. Nature of stay: 1) Alone   2) With family or relatives   3) With Peers
                 4) Others (specify) _____
18. If you stay alone then do you have contact with your family members?   1) Yes   2)No
3)NA
19. If 'Yes', frequency of visit in week _____ Month _____ Year

20. How long have you been staying without your family (total duration)?
_____

B: - Personal Health & Hygiene:

21. 1. Do you brush your teeth?   Yes / No;   2.   Frequency/   week:
_____;
     3. Nature of brushing agent _____
22. 1. Place of defecation: Open air/ Toilet;   2. Hand washing after that? Yes / No
     3.   Washing   agent?

23. 1. Frequency of bathing/ week: _____;   2.Use soap? Yes / No;
     3. If yes, frequency/day _____ / week _____ /
month_____

24. 1. Do you take your regular meals (lunch & dinner)?   Yes / No;
    2. Frequency of regular meal for last
3days:_____

25. 1. If No; then what do you take?
_____;
    2. Reason for not taking above meals:
_____

26. How do you manage hunger? 1. Suppress hunger   2.Discarded food   3. Begging
food   4. Stealing food
5.Others_____
27. Place of taking food: 1) At home   2) Public place   3) Private place owned by
others
                            4) Others
_____

28. 1. How many times had you taken fish / egg/ meat for last 3days?   Yes / No;
    2. If 'No' then how
frequently_____
29. Where do you go during minor illness
_____

30. Status of immunization indicated by BCG scar mark: Yes / No

C: - History related to violence/injury:

31. Did you have any harassment/ assault within last 6 months?   Y / N;
32. 1. If yes, by whom
_____
    2. Frequency /day_____ / week_____ month
_____
33. Nature of harassment & perceived reason:
_____
34. 1. Do you remember any sequel following assault?   Yes/ No;   2. If yes, nature of
it:
    1) Physical   2) Mental   3) Both
35. Have you ever had any conflicts among yourselves for sharing OF food, shelter, recreation
etc? Yes/ No
36. 1. Nature of conflicts: Verbal argument / Threatening / Physical assault;
    2. Frequency in a month:
_____
37. 1. Did you face physical injury related to this?   Yes/ No;
    2. How it was solved?
_____
38. If you had been sufficiently injured, did you take treatment facility?   Y / N;
    2) By
whom?_____
39. Had police take any action against the culprit?   Y / N
40. Have you ever been arrested or kept in remand home/s within last one year due to any
crime?

Y / N

41. If yes, what kind of crime committed by you?
_____

42. Attitude of general people towards you: 1) Well accepted   2) Indifferent   3) Hatred
                                              4) Not known

43. 1. Do you face any harassment at your working place?   Yes / No / NA;
    2. Nature of it: Physical / Mental / Both

D: - History of Substance Abuse:

44. 1. Do you have smoking habits?   Yes/ No;   2.   Age   of   initiation:
    _____;
    3. Frequency/day: _____
45. Are you currently taking any drug/chemical substance?   Yes / No
46. Name the substances:
_____

47. 1. Age of first taking substance: _____
    2. Reason of taking
substance_____
48. 1. Frequency of consumption of substance/s: _____;
    2. Cost for substance abuse/day: _____
49. 1. Total drug taking duration: _____   2. Continuously / Intermittently
50. Do you consume it: 1) Alone   2) In a group   3) Both
51. If you consume it in a group, then average no of partners during addiction:
_____

52. Do you have fixed partner for addiction?   Yes / No;
53. If no, then with how many different persons you enjoyed addiction within last ?weeks?
_____

    54. Route of addiction preferred: 1) Oral   2) Inhalation   3) IM
        4) IV
                              5) Others (specify)
_____

55. Why do you prefer that route?
_____

56. From where did you get money to support your habit?
_____

57. If you do not have money then how do you manage to get drugs?___
_____

58. Who assisted you to initiate this habit
_____

59. Do you feel increasing sexual urge after taking substances? Yes / No / No idea / No
response
 60. Have you ever faced any health problem/s related to substance use? Yes / No;
61. If 'Yes' then specify: 1) Withdrawal   2. Insomnia   3. Anorexia

62. Have you ever received any treatment for this? Yes / No
63. If 'Yes' then from where did you get such treatment?
_____

64. Have you ever received any counseling?   Yes / No

E: - History of Sexual Abuse (Unwillingly):

65. Do you recall any episode of sexual harassment within last 1 year, that means-
   1) Anybody hugged you forcefully?   Yes / No;
      If yes then
frequency_____
   2) Anybody kissed you forcefully?   Yes / No;
      If yes then
frequency_____
   3) Anybody exposed his/ her genitalia to you?   Yes / No;
      If yes then
frequency_____
   4) Anybody forced to expose your genitalia to him/ her?   Yes / No;
      If yes then
frequency_____
   5) Anybody touched your genitalia forcefully?   Yes / No;
      If yes then
frequency_____
   6) Anybody forced you to touch his/ her genitalia?   Yes / No;
      If yes then
frequency_____
   7) Anybody forced you to sit on his/ her lap?   Yes / No:
      If yes then
frequency_____
   8) Anybody tried to have sex with you?   Yes / No;
      If yes then frequency_____
   9) Anybody forcefully had penetrative-sex with you?   Yes / No;
      1. Oral   2. Anal   3. Vaginal;
      Frequency_____
66. If you are abused / harassed sexually then mention the frequency of this maltreatment within
      last 1yr: _____
67. Were you abused by: 1) Single person, Single occassion   2) Single persons, multiple
                        Occassion   3) Multiple persons, multiple occassion
68. Can you remember the age of your first sexual harassment (unwillingly)?
      (Specify) _____

F: - Sexual Practices (Willingly):

69. Do you have any physical relationship with your friend/ partner/ lover?   Y / N
70. 1. Have you ever had penetrative sex with any of them?   Yes/ No;
    2. Frequency: _____
71. 1. If no, then have you had non-penetrative sex any time?   Yes/ No;

    2. Frequency: _____
72. 1. Do you need to go for sex working to earn money (for females only)?   Y / N
    2. If yes, then duration of work _____
    3. No. of clients /day_____
73.1. Did you have any sexual act at time of menstruation?   Yes / No;

2. if yes then frequency_____
74.1. Have you ever visited sex workers within last one year?   Y / N;
    2. If Yes then frequency _____
75. Do you have male sex partner? (In case of male participant):   Yes / No
76. Have you ever performed anal sex with your partner?   Yes / No
77. Do you perform it as an: 1) Active partner,   2) Receptor,   3) Both
78.1. Have you ever used condom?   Yes / No;
    2. Frequency: 1) Always,   2) Frequently,   3) Sometimes,   4) Rarely

79.1. If yes, then why? _____ ;
    2. If no, then why? _____ ;
80.1. Have you ever suffered from any kind of STD within last one year?   Yes / No;
    2. If yes, then: 1. Ulcer   2. Discharge
81. If yes, where did you go for treatment?
_____

G: - Knowledge:

82. Have you ever heard about HIV/AIDS?   Yes / No
83. How HIV is transmitted?   1) Unsafe sex,   2) Contaminated needle-syringe,
                                   3) Unsafe blood transfusion,   4) Mother to child,
                                   5) Not Known   6) No Response
84. How HIV is prevented?   1) Using condom during sex,   2) Using disposable needle-
syringe,
                                   3) Safe blood transfusion,   4) Not Known   5) No
                    Response
85. Can a healthy looking person be HIV positive?   Yes / No / Not Known / NR
86. Do you feel that you are at risk of acquiring HIV due to your street life?
    1. Yes   2. No   3. Not Known   4. No Response
87. How did you learn it? _____

Signature of Interviewer

LIST OF PUBLICATIONS

List of Publications:

1. K. Sarkar, S. Mitra, B. Bal et al. *Rapid spread of Hepatitis C and needle exchange programme in Kolkata, India.* Lancet 2003; 361: 1301-02.

2. K. Sarkar, D. N. Ganguly, B. Bal, M. K. Saha, S. K. Bhattacharya et. al. *Hepatitis B Infection, Eastern India.* Emerging Infectious Diseases, Vol. 10, No.7, July 2004.

3. Kamalesh Sarkar, Baisali Bal, Rita Mukherjee, Swapan Kumar Niyogi, Malay Kumar Saha & Sujit Kumar Bhattacharya. *Cross-border HIV epidemic among IDUs of Himalayan West Bengal.* Eur J Epidemiol (2005) vol.20 (4); 373-374

4. Kamalesh Sarkar, Baisali Bal, Rita Mukherjee, Swapan Kumar Niyogi, Malay Kumar Saha & Sujit Kumar Bhattacharya. *Epidemiology of HIV in brothel based sex workers of Kolkata city.* J HEALTH POPUL NUTR, 2005 Sep; 23(3): 231-235

5. Kamalesh Sarkar, Baisali Bal, Rita Mukherjee, Swapan Kumar Niyogi, Malay Kumar Saha & Sujit Kumar Bhattacharya. *Epidemic of HIV coupled with HCV among Injecting Drug Users of Himalayan West Bengal, eastern India, Bordering Nepal, Bhutan & Bangladesh.* Journal of Substance Use & Misuse,2006 Nov; 41(3):341-352.

6. Kamalesh Sarkar, Baishali Bal, Rita Mukherjee, Malay Kumar Saha, Sekhar Chakraborty, Swapan Kumar Niyogi and Sujit Kumar Bhattacharya. *Young age is a risk factor for HIV among female sex workers – an experience from India.* Journal of Infection (2006); 53(4): 255-59.

7. Baishali Bal, S.I. Ahmed, Rita Mukherjee, Sekhar Chakraborty, Swapan Kumar Niyogi, Arunagsu Talukder, Nilanjan Chakraborty and Kamalesh Sarkar. *HIV infection among transport workers operating through Siliguri-Guwahati national highway, India.* J INT ASSOC PHYSICIANS AIDS CARE 6(1); 2007

8. Kamalesh Sarkar, Baishali Bal, Rita Mukherjee, Sekhar Chakraborty, Suman Saha, Arundhuti Ghosh and Scot Parsons. *Sex trafficking, violence, negotiating skill and HIV infection in brothel-based sex workers of eastern India, adjoining Nepal, Bhutan & Bangladesh;* J HEALTH POPUL NUTR 2008 Jun; 26(2):223-231

9. Kamalesh Sarkar, Swati Bhattacharya et. al. *Oncogenic Human Papilloma Virus and cervical pre-cancerous lesion in brothel-based sex workers of India.* Journal of Infection & Public Health (2008); 1: 121 – 128.

10. Kamalesh Sarkar, Rita Mukherjee, Sekhar Chakraborty, Swapan Kumar Niyogi and Baishali Bal. *Epidemiology of HIV and sexually transmitted infections in sex workers of West Bengal; Proceedings of conference on Recent Advances and Challenges in Reproductive Health Research,* 19 – 21 February 2007, published by Indian Council of Medical Research, New Delhi (2008) 207 - 221.

11. Kamalesh Sarkar, Santa sabuj Das, Reshmi Pal, Baishali Bal, P. Madhusudan and Sekhar Chakraborti. *HIV Infection and Host Genetic Mutation among Injecting Drug-users of Northeastern States of India;* J HEALTH POPUL NUTR, 2010 Apr; 28(2): 130-136.

12. Subhajit Bhattacharjee, sayantani Bhattacharjee, Baishali Bal, Reshmi Pal, Swapan Kumar Niyogi and Kamalesh sarkar. *Is Vibrio fluvialis Emerging as a pathogen with Epidemic Potential in Coastal Region of Eastern India Following Cyclone Aila?* J HEALTH POPUL NUTR, 2010 Aug; 28(4): 311-317.

13. Baishali Bal, Rupa Mitra, Aiyel H. Mallick, Sekhar Chakraborti and Kamalesh sarkar. *Non-tobacco substance abuse, sexual abuse, HIV & sexually Transmitted Infection among street children in Kolkata, India;* Substance use & Misuse, 2010 Aug; 45(10): 1668-1682.

Lightning Source UK Ltd.
Milton Keynes UK
176763UK00001B/96/P